BRITISH RAILWA

PAST and PRESENT

No 14

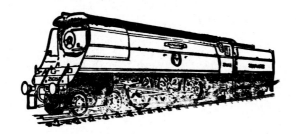

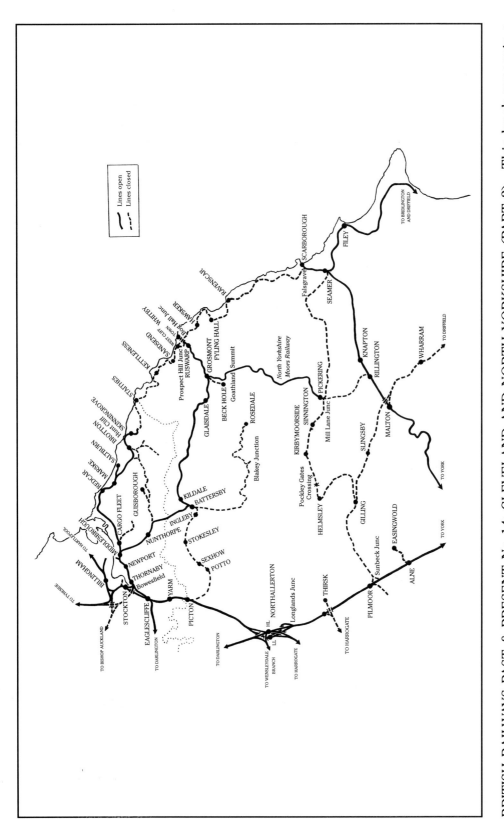

BRITISH RAILWAYS PAST & PRESENT No 14: CLEVELAND AND NORTH YORKSHIRE (PART 2) - This book presents a detailed examination of the changing face of the railways in the region depicted in this map, which includes locations featured in the photographs or mentioned in the text. The pictures have been chosen to provide a balanced view, including railways which are still in use or being developed, together with scenes where the lines have been closed and either abandoned or redeveloped since the 'past' pictures were taken.

BRITISH RAILWAYS

PAST and PRESENT

No 14

Cleveland and North Yorkshire
(Part 2)

Alan R. Thompson & Ken Groundwater

SLP

Silver Link Publishing Ltd

Copyright © Alan R. Thompson and Ken Groundwater
1992

First published in July 1992

British Library Cataloguing in Publication Data

British Railways Past and Present.
No 14: Cleveland and North Yorkshire. Part 2
     I. Thompson, Alan R.
     II. Groundwater, Ken
     385.0941

ISBN 0 947971 84 X

Silver Link Publishing Ltd
The Trundle
Ringstead Road
Great Addington
Kettering
Northants NN14 4BW

Maps drawn by Christina Siviter

Printed and bound in Great Britain by
Woolnough Bookbinding Ltd, Irthlingborough, Northants

NOTE: Photographs credited JWA were taken by J. W.
Armstrong, ART by Alan R. Thompson and KG by Ken
Groundwater, while those credited BR appear by courtesy
of British Railways. All other credits are given in full.

'We were taken from the ore bed and the mine
We were melted in the furnace and the pit
We were cast and wrought and hammered to design
We were cut and filed and tooled and gauged to fit'

The Secret of the Machines, Rudyard Kipling

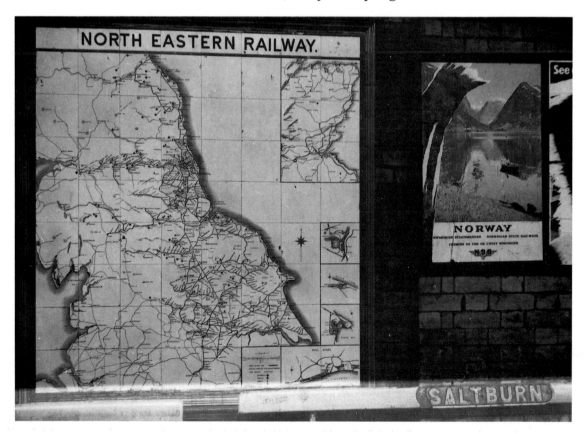

NER tile map, Saltburn, 1959. *JWA*

CONTENTS

ACKNOWLEDGEMENTS

Acknowledgements go to the remaining members of the John W. Armstrong Trust who have fully cooperated in ensuring that John's fine record of both Durham and Yorkshire has been seen to the best advantage.

John Midcalf, Peter J. Robinson, Dave Tyreman, Ken Linford and John Boyes gave invaluable assistance with photography and advice. The author Ken Appleby assisted with S&D matters; Trevor J. Ermel helped via his business 'Monochrome'; whilst Phil Atkins, Librarian at the NRM, York, turned up the remarkable Blakey Junction print (page 86). Thanks also to Tees-side railwaymen Fred Noble (who incidentally retired in 1991 - we wish him well), Norman Alexander and Stephen Shields.

We would also like to thank Peter Mountain and, before him, Martin Idale, successive Area Managers of the Tees-Tyne freight area, and David Judson, of the equivalent Regional Railways area, for their assistance with facilities and topical information.

BIBLIOGRAPHY

The Scarborough & Whitby Railway by Robin Lidster (Hendon Publications)
Railway Stations of the North-East by K. Hoole (David & Charles)
The Railways of Ryedale by Patrick Howatt (Hendon Publications)
The Pilmoor, Boroughbridge and Knaresborough Railway by Patrick Howatt (M. Bairstow)
Rosedale Mines & Railways by Hayes and Rutter (Scarborough History Society)
What Happened to Steam (various editions) by P.B. Hands
Locomotives of the LNER (various parts) (RCTS)
North Eastern Record by various NERA authors (HMRS)
Shildon - Newport in Retrospect by Ken Appleby (RCTS)
Railways around Whitby by Martin Bairstow (M. Bairstow)
The NER: Its Rise and Development by W.W. Tomlinson (David & Charles)
NER Locomotive Sheds by Paul Bolger (Ian Allan)

SOUTH BANK, MIDDLESBROUGH: Conjuring up memories of some of Colin Gifford's spectacular industrial imagery of the early 1960s in this area and seen at a time when 'green' meant the colour of the stagnant residue ponds in and around Cargo Fleet, we see Class 'J25' No 65720 of 51D, Middlesbrough MPD, shunting near mineral wool products sidings against a backcloth of South Bank Coke/Steel Works in 1956. *K. Linford*

The coke ovens survive today against all the odds, and the associated steel plant (to the left) looks much smarter without the pall of smoke, to the extent of having a whitewashed face. Class '37' No 37110 leaves the yard with a train of lime empties in March 1990. The small 'J25' mineral engine survived longer that most of its sisters and became one of the last eight by January 1962, eventually being cut up at Darlington Works in May of that year after more than 50 years' service in and around the steel works of Tees-side. *ART*

INTRODUCTION

This is an area of deep industrial tradition wherein families still boast of a lineage back to Stockton & Darlington roots or connections with the great 'ironmasters' of the 19th century. It cannot be disputed that, in industrial terms, the area certainly made an impression nationally and the railway, as the 'father', the catalyst, was eventually eclipsed by the 'child' or, to put in bluntly, one hundred furnaces that lit the Yorkshire night skies like the Northern Lights. Railway stories from the area abound, but one in particular tells us that during an (early) inter-Union dispute the loyalty of railwaymen here was hard pressed and resulted in someone (from the LNWR?) coining them 'pease-pudding men', clearly reflecting the influence of one remarkable Quaker family upon the workforce and the area.

This is perhaps something of an understatement as it was Edward Pease who facilitated the eventual growth of Tees-side when, viewing a cluster of buildings at a place called Middlesbrough Farm, he said 'Some day we will export coal from here - some-day. . .', eventually steering the 'Middlesbrough Owners' into securing more than 500 acres that became the nucleus of the town.

What came over strong during our area study were the incredible contradictions within a relatively small corner of England; contradictions not only in landscape but in the way that man's labours are intensified all the more by the fact that chemist and steelmaster share the neighbourhood with farmer and fisherman. At one extreme, smuggling was still an upwardly mobile occupation within sight of the first blast furnaces, and speed trials to break world records were held on Saltburn 'flats' whilst collier brig construction continued within Whitby's 'haven under the hill'. Some of these long-past, and not-so-long-past, activities (ironstone mining ceased at North Skelton as recently as 1964) help to make Cleveland and North Yorkshire most fascinating subjects for this sort of 'time travel' study (but also frustrating in having to stick to a fixed transport theme!).

At Scarborough the now well-known LNER posters haunted revisitings, whilst along the south bank of the Tees Colin Gifford's and Malcolm Dunnett's evocative 1960s 'shades of grey' style of photography accentuated the now vast void in our current manufacturing ability - as well as the cleaner environment! A journey from, say, Middlesbrough to Redcar still today serves to give a last glimpse of a way of life that was once so common in the Iron North, for the section between South Bank and British Steel continues to give a superb vignette of the fire and brimstone world that built the British Empire; whereupon making an exit from this 'dark tubular tunnel', the entry (and contrast) into genteel Redcar is quite a culture shock!

Journeys along such rail corridors sharply focus the subtle and mysterious passage in time, which although occurring almost imperceptibly is, even as we read, gathering momentum to make each 'yesterday' a part of a developing 'trend' that, when looked at from over our shoulders, surprises those even in Helmsley, who maintain that 'nothing ever happens here'! Only time makes the gap significant and, for their pains in identifying trends early, marketing managers are often paid disproportionate fees just to tell us how we should behave (and respond) to fit in tomorrow!

Perhaps this is a perverse sort of introduction to what may be considered 'just' a book of railway pictures, but none of the books in this series has been 'just' railways! For the discerning observer the peripheral scene, especially around stations, says so much more. It is here that we see a complete cross-section of life at the time, via social habits, costume, materials in use, architecture; all joined forces to shape the world as we know it now.

In our case the railway theme has been an excellent vehicle for recording not only the main but also the peripheral change because, happily, so many photographers were drawn to point their cameras only vaguely at trains, for which we are especially grateful today. This is borne out by the fact that local and general historians rely more than ever on the work of someone like John Armstrong, as he showed particular stamina in maintaining a record of changes over more than 40 years that embraced great latitude.

Level crossings seemed to have been his forte, and are especially rich for showing 'side-show' details. Look at the old half-cab bus *en route* for Ripon on page 68, and see the then common tandem cycle at the gates at Potto (page 74). Even more remarkable from today's stance on safety is the unprotected open-top tractor delayed by the gates at Picton (page 73) - then totally acceptable on a public highway (but, of course, 60 mph then was 'pushing it'!).

A new theme for us was finding the signalman at both Malton and Scarborough 'present' was also featured at Rillington 'past' - but perhaps we'll leave that book subject for someone else!

It only remains now for readers to look at the site of the world's first passenger-carrying railway terminus against the backdrop of Europe's largest petro-chemical plant, then compare it with Rosedale's inhospitable table-top railway and the not so very distant sylvan setting found at Pockley Gates, in beautiful Ryedale's lush vale. There can then be little doubt that 'contradiction' very suitably describes the area within.

Ken Groundwater
Gateshead
Alan R. Thompson
Penshaw, Co Durham

Notes on previous adjoining volumes
Certain locations north of the Tees have been incorporated which were omitted from 'Past and Present' No 4, and several from the Durham side rightly objected! We apologise to these people and will now be in bigger trouble when they find that they are lumped together with what is essentially a 'Yorkshire' book!

An addenda to our perhaps now over-optimistic comments in 'Past and Present' No 11 concerns the Wensleydale branch. The fact that the Wensleydale Rail Association were close to examining lease/lend arrangements for some form of motive power to institute a limited Summer service along the branch gave rise to optimism, but in February 1992 came the bombshell for all in this area that British Steel was withdrawing arrangements with BR for the haulage of the 1,800-plus tonnes - consequently dooming the branch for further rail activities as the sole sponsor. An article in *RAIL* in the same month reported that a mere 3 per cent difference was the 'quibble', consigning up to 60 lorries daily to damage the dale's already groaning roads.

Fortunately, and perhaps due to the looming election of 1992, this hot environmental issue resulted in a stay of execution, for a further six months. Time will tell if common sense will prevail, as uplifted lines over this distance rarely get replaced, and North Yorkshire Moors-type stamina for rail revival is all too uncommon!

CLEVELAND

Billingham and Stockton

BILLINGHAM ICI: Our opening Cleveland view shows a red letter day for ICI, as the first consignment of iso-octanol prepares to leave the sidings of the heavy organic chemicals division *en route* for Melbourne, Australia, via London's King George V Docks and the SS *Afric*. 300 tons of the chemical, a plasticiser alcohol, left Billingham in 19 tank wagons behind Darlington-based Class 'B1s' Nos 61304 and 61034 on 4 March 1961, and the plant continued to grow and grow thereafter. *BR*

Much has changed in what today is a heavily-guarded security area. The never-ending bucket chain has gone but it can be seen that much else has sprung up in what is a constantly changing process. The sidings are known to railwayman as the 'grids' with tank wagons today much changed, the most notable difference being the UN 'hazard' code descriptions with emergency and even first aid recommendations for all to see - no longer can the contents remain secret. *KG*

Although the **Stockton & Darlington Railway** was not really the first railway to convey passengers (the Oystermouth Railway is accepted as achieving this first), it is generally accepted that its first train of public passengers and drawn by steam on 27 September 1825 was the technological breakthrough for which all others were waiting in the wings. If the enterprising S&D Board had not brought together the cocktail of Stephenson, Wood and Hackworth then it may have been many more years before steam railways finally ousted waterborne competition.

The S&D was fundamentally a prototype and acted as a springboard for more commercially enterprising concerns, which learned from its mistakes. The Liverpool & Manchester took the lead by 1830 when it banned private contractors from using its tracks and began operating a dedicated steam railway for both passengers and freight - the railway age had really begun!

The meeting between Edward Pease (already an old retired gentleman) and Stephenson on 28 April 1821 is generally accepted as the date when Stephenson's common-sense argument for steam locomotion over waterways and horse traction caused Pease to stop in his tracks. The result was the line from Etherley to Stockton St Johns that opened in 1825. We are fortunate to have found a very early view of the historic location where the first rails were laid back on 23 May 1822 (six months before the Hetton Colliery Railway opened!).

STOCKTON (ST JOHN'S WELL CROSSING), the location where the first rails were ceremoniously laid for the start of the Stockton & Darlington Railway on 23 May 1822 by Thomas Meynell. Seen (*above left*) *circa* 1900, the first view demonstrates the already uncared-for working goods railway conditions into which this cradle of all railways degenerated. The S&D station building is already leaning to the right due to subsidence and the tall chimney is optimistically held by wire to the roof. Note the spacious fogging hut with finial on the left. The arrival of the Leeds Northern in 1853 using the new route through the present-day Stockton station relegated this branch to very definitely freight-only! Its original S&D purpose was for the transportation of coal down to the wharf on the River Tees shipment. The Middlesbrough extension of 1830 diverging at Bowesfield saw Pease's dream of deep-river exports come true, but killed Stockton Wharf for anything barring lightweight shipments. *BR*

Seen again (*left*) in the mid to late 1950s, the NER finialed signal has been replaced by a BR steel pole, but an original NER semaphore signal remains alongside the now much cleaner wheel-cabin across on the other side of Bridge Road. It is pleasing to see in the condition of the station area that someone had begun to take pride in their unique heritage at that time. Across Bridge Street it can be seen that a Shellmex 45-ton tank wagon occupies still active sidings towards Moat Street, but time was now rapidly running out for the Stockton Wharf branch and by 1967 it was closed to rail traffic for ever - ending 142 years of operation. *JWA*

On 13 March 1992 (*above*), poised at a crazy angle and with a signboard reading DANGEROUS BUILDING - KEEP CLEAR, the station is surely awaiting a decision that may end its days. A lot now depends upon Stockton Town Council and the various benevolent heritage trusts to save this auspicious site. The course of the line is well mapped out as the 'S&D Trail', and a plaque on the house wall together with a trailway educational display sets the scene. The house wall plaque states: 'HERE IN 1825 THE STOCKTON AND DARLINGTON RAILWAY COMPANY BOOKED THE FIRST PASSENGER THUS MARKING AN EPOCH IN THE HISTORY OF MANKIND'. *KG*

We are told that '. . .the Company's first "moveable engine" [*Locomotion*] arrived from Stephenson's Works in Newcastle hauled by three horse-drawn carts in the middle of September 1825, and was unloaded at Aycliffe Lane. Unfortunately it is said that there was no means of lighting the engine and Stephenson was just about to send a man off for a candle when a workman called Robert Metcalf stepped forward with his magnifying glass (which he said he often used to light his pipe) and then lit up some material for the fire. . .' Sad to relate, *Locomotion* failed after a few days and it took the best of Hackworth's men to get it in working order - almost rebuilding it!

The rest, as they say, is history, and as a tribute to Edward Pease we have included a photograph of a loco that was constructed when engines were tried and tested in a more reliable manner!

Derwent was constructed by the firm of A. Kitching of Darlington in 1845, and was regularly seen around the Stockton Wharf area in the early years. So impressed were the Pease family that they purchased *Derwent* for the family business. In 1898 Pease and Partners presented it back to the NER who displayed her here at Darlington until she became entrusted to the care of the National Railway Museum at York. *BR*

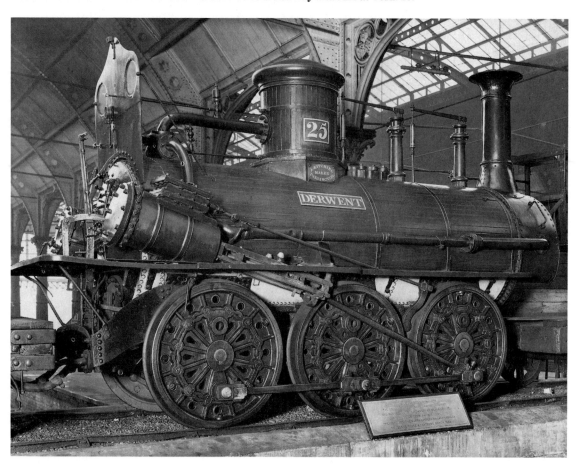

STOCKTON WHARF BRANCH (MOAT STREET): After the first historic train journey down the S&D line from Etherley on 27 September 1825, it was reported that engine No 1 *Locomotion* and the vehicles forming the train were put on public display here in a position near the end of Moat Street and adjoining Brougham Street - about half a mile from the end of the Wharf branch. The following pictures of this area are *circa* 1930 and serve to show the appalling conditions endured by the folks living down near the Tees. It may be thought that the mud was a result of heavy rain, but the truth is that these wharflands at Stockton were subject to tidal overflows from an, as yet, unrestrained River Tees. In this first picture it seems that a woman is crouched attempting to clear seaweed and river debris from her door! *BR*

On 13 March 1992 we can see that Stockton's planners had no love for bits of useless historic railway, and the remains of Moat Street were demolished in the early 1970s to pave the way for this inner bypass now running along the actual path of the old S&D for about a mile. *KG*

STOCKTON WHARF BRANCH (FINKLE STREET): Almost half a mile to the north of Moat Street the S&D Wharf Branch began skirting the Tees approaching the Quay shipping point adjacent to Finkle Street - the street name of which can be seen on the building to the right. Finkle Street ran down to Calverts Lane along which the branch ran in (by 1930) quite squalid conditions. As with our previous view, Calverts Lane was the subject of uncertain tidal conditions which must have resulted in NER permanent way staff studying the tides to plan maintenance possessions! A feeling of Depression comes over as we see two men standing outside the door of Wright & Sons - Marine Stockists - perhaps hopeful of work. Other groups of men are dotted about along the lane leading towards the Moat Street area. Over on the right is advertised (to those in work) Cameron's Sparkling Ales. *BR*

In March 1992 Calverts Lane is an urban bypass and, as luck would have it, it was the opposite side of Finkle Street that was left standing by the town planners! We therefore also turn through about 40 degrees from the same spot to look up the remains of Finkle Street (*above*) wherein we can in some way imagine the incredible clean-up operation that has been undertaken. *Both KG*

STOCKTON S&D WHARF: The aspirations of the early S&D Board plans got no further than here, the Wharf at Stockton Corporation Quay at the bottom of old Silver Street. This was to have been where a million tons of South Durham steam coal would have been shipped to the rest of the British Empire. As part of the learning process of this prototype railway it quickly became evident that the draught of the Tees here would see little expansion in vessel size - and thus payload - and Pease quickly began plans for his Middlesbrough extension that would herald the birth of the latter place. This extraordinary view, thought to be in September 1947, shows a line-up of four ages in transport evolution: the primitive hand-cart, a new Leyland lorry (with pneumatic tyres, a great advance on the wooden cart wheels), an industrial tank engine and, just out of view, a coaster receiving what may be a dolomite load, as seen stockpiled beyond. Over to the left is a Magnet Ales Brewery to which it seems the lorry may belong. Details regarding the little tank are interesting. It is a Black Hawthorn 0-4-0 built in 1877, Works No 477. It seems to have been ordered by the Tyne-Tees Shipping Company for work here and was simply named *Push*. It had an older sister called *Pull* built at Fletcher Jennings Works in the year 1867 and sold (for scrap?) in 1949. *Push* saw work here until 1955 when it was made redundant. *John M. Boyes Collection*

The March 1992 view really is the same place! It was with some local help that the Corporation Quay was definitely identified, and with some astonishment that in a place like Stockton one can go for a stroll along a promenade! Today's clean lines and uncluttered environs contrast sharply with the huddle of yesteryear, but it can be seen that coasters have maintained the business created by the S&D and Edward Pease so long ago, and the railway is remembered via Heritage Trail storyboards along the quay walk. *KG*

South Tees-side and Middlesbrough

EAGLESCLIFFE: Although geographically on the 1825 S&D route, the location was not named as such. It appeared on the map in 1852, courtesy of the newly formed junction with the Leeds Northern Railway and was known as Preston Junction; the two railways kept rigidly to their own side of the platform (from the viewpoint shown, the S&D utilised the far face of the island platform, whilst the near side was the domain of the LNR). This view, looking north-east in the summer of 1965, shows the station's £13,000 reconstruction of 1893, which resulted in the large canopy and improved station facilities. A Darlington-bound DMU is seen at the LNR side whilst a relatively new Class '37' stands alongside a Class '24' diesel. *JWA*

Returning today, it strikes the observer that facilities must have returned to something closely akin to the pre-1893 conditions following the trimming allied to 'unstaffed' status. The old goods yard office alone survives in splendid isolation adjacent to the car park. It is January 1990 and the limestone hoppers for Redmire, along the Wensleydale branch (see 'Past and Present' No 11) are led south towards Picton (see page 73) by Class '37' Nos 668 *Redmire* and 508, both from the Thornaby Fleet Engineer's Metal pool. By the time this book is on sale we should know if these trains will continue beyond the currently planned cessation date of 30 September 1992! *ART*

BOWESFIELD: These shots are included especially for those who complained about the omission of this important junction from 'Past and Present' No 4. A Class 'V1' 2-6-2 tank engine is seen leading a Middlesbrough-Newcastle service towards the northern apex of the triangular junction via Stockton Cut, to join the Leeds Northern route at Hartburn Junction. The stock includes several displaced ECML corridor coaches and suburban 'slam doors' to the rear. It seems as if the LNER has been guilty of some 'duplicity' if the proximity of the two large gantries means anything! Former regular passengers on the Darlington and Newcastle routes will well remember the imposing and well-advertised mass of Davy, Ashmore, Benson, Pease & Co Ltd. *JWA*

The latter building was removed in the late '80s, and the collection of signalling equipment is now summarised by two unobtrusive white location boxes and a small gantry in a new position; however, the nerve centre of junction operations remains Bowesfield signal cabin, untouched, as yet, by the creeping fingers of IECC (electronic) signalling. In March 1990 a Class '143' 'Pacer' enjoys its final years on these North East routes, for by the time of publication the Newcastle-Middlesbrough service will be in the hands of the more appropriately appointed 'Sprinter' units; the '143s' should by then have been transferred to South Wales, and shorter hauls. *ART*

The additional view (*above*) from just outside Bowesfield box is interesting for several reasons. First of all it was recorded on 26 March 1987, just days before the large building was demolished and the landscape here changed dramatically for ever. Also caught in the throes of recovery are the remaining point rods and a now bare gantry (a close look at the main 'past' photo shows all 17 rod slots occupied). One for the modern traction enthusiast, the photograph shows No 37501 *Teesside Steelmaster*, wearing her unique coat of powder blue, together with more orthodox No 37512 bringing train 4E35, the Grange-Lackenby, home. *Peter J. Robinson*

Situated to the east of Thornaby Station and west of the Old Newport Yards, **Thornaby MPD** was constructed during 1957 in order to bring some order and organisation to the ramshackle engine maintenance facilities that had existed for possibly far too long at both Newport and Middlesbrough. Opened in June 1958, Thornaby depot had first-class maintenance equipment designed with the eventual disposition towards the total diesel era in mind. After the first year of opening, in July 1959, the allocation looked like this: 6 Class '4MT'; 32 Class 'Q6'; 42 Class 'J26'; 4 Class 'A5'; 4 Class 'J71'; 4 Class 'J94'; 5 Class 'L1'; 9 Class 'J72'; 5 Class 'A8'; 30 Class 'WD' 2-8-0; plus some single representatives of other classes, giving an impressive allocation of 147.

THORNABY MPD (1): Our first picture (*above*) shows two Class 'J72s' standing at the far road of the fire drop and wash-out area on the northern fringe of the depot. No 69007 had spent the late '50s at Sunderland before going (briefly) to West Auckland and Darlington, becoming a Thornaby engine in 1961. It is seen in October 1961, a year before condemnation and cutting up at Darlington Works. No 69017 was withdrawn before its sister - April 1962 - and remained in store at Thornaby until September of that year, when it made the journey to Darlington scrap yard. *ART*

In April 1990 the area is occupied by condemned diesels and the Thornaby-maintained snow ploughs. Beyond the surviving separating railings lie the west end departure sidings of the main yard area. Then recently transferred Class '37' No 37415 can be seen passing, still in Scotrail livery. *KG*

THORNABY MPD (2): The second view at the west end and looking towards Thornaby station - just visible - illustrates a spread of those most 'North Eastern' engines, the Class 'Q6' 0-8-0s. No 63375 appears far too clean for a common mineral engine and seems to have recently returned from a Darlington Works overhaul. She was a Middlesbrough (51D) engine until that shed closed, then coming to Thornaby, staying here until 1962 - a year after this picture date. She then moved to West Auckland, being withdrawn in August 1963. Adjacent is No 63341. She came to Thornaby in 1959 from West Auckland, returned in 1962 and was withdrawn in November 1964. Furthest from the camera is No 63370, a Newport engine until Thornaby opened in June 1958. She left 51L in November 1962, being transferred to Leeds Neville Hill, and was withdrawn in June 1964. The trio were all cut up at Darlington Works. *ART*

Today at the same location the ladder of tracks occupied by No 63370 has been removed - the semaphores in the distance have long gone, but the floodlights, with a taller addition, remain as 'markers'. The area is used by the fleet engineer as a storage location at the blind side of the depot. A cannibalised Class '08' No 08200, a DMU power car and a long-withdrawn Class '45' (latterly a departmental Class '97') patiently await disposal. *KG*

THORNABY MPD (3): This third view takes in a wide area at the west end showing (centre) the four-road 'wash-out' shed, a sprawl of mineral wagons beyond in the area that became Tees yard and, to the right, the four-road preparation and disposal shed. Over the 12-road spread at this point could often be seen up to 60 engines, especially during summer weekends during the colliery holidays - a veritable spotters' paradise! *ART*

It can be seen that, following the demise of steam in December 1964, the area was revamped into an efficient diesel locomotive maintenance area, retaining facilities for carriage and wagon repairs in what was the steam heavy maintenance shed. By April 1990 the sprawling Tees Yard has risen and declined at the mercy of the fickle mineral business, surviving only due to the more buoyant metal-haulage contracts with British Steel. Thornaby is in consequence the home of Railfreight's Metals Sector Area Fleet Engineer, still, in 1991, receiving delivery of brand new Class '60s' planned eventually to eclipse the now ageing fleet of Thornaby Class '37s'. *KG*

NEWPORT MPD: The shed area was difficult to define as it stood engulfed by Newport's extensive marshalling yard network. Perhaps as a result of 1930s economies the main shed buildings of 1890 fell rapidly into disrepair culminating in the eventual collapse of some roof area in early 1939, sadly killing a member of staff. This 1950 view of the east end of the shed from the depot's only external turntable shows a preponderance of ugly but functional 'WD' Class engines. Amongst others, No 90230 stands ahead of No 90074 with No 90132 at the extreme right and Class '06' No 63360 at the end of another road of 'WDs'. *F. W. Hampson*

Cleared during 1959, following closure in June of the previous year, the site made way for the modernised and more concentrated freight handling facilities known as Tees yard. Newport's allocation, including almost all of the remaining Class 'J26' locomotives, was transferred *en masse* to the new Thornaby depot close by. Seen today from the nearest practical viewpoint, the area is straddled by the busy central motorway held aloft near Newport East Junction. It can be seen that Newport Bridge (the first vertical lift bridge of its kind in the country) is the only recurring theme but for a vaguely discerned gasholder to the right of the bridge. Tees yard is laid waste at this point today following the decline in the traditional heavy industries of Tees-side, but the more active west end lies in wait for the upsurge in rail's contribution to national freight haulage as predicted by the Rt Hon Malcolm Rifkind MP (as a result of privatisation?). *ART*

NEWPORT EAST JUNCTION: The Tees transporter bridge is glimpsed between two gasholders as Class 'Q6' 0-8-0 No 63407 raises the echoes amongst the serried house rows in this older part of Middlesbrough. Evidently hauling coal empties for return to the Durham pits, this engine spent most of her career 'south of the Wear' (ie Sunderland). In 1958 she was based at Haverton Hill, being transferred the following year to West Auckland and in 1964 moving on to West Hartlepool, becoming one of the last survivors. Going into store at Hartlepool from July to October 1967, she was eventually towed up to Tyneside and was cut up by Clayton & Davie at Dunston-on-Tyne in November 1967.

Coal empties continue to pass Newport East Junction today, and on 31 May 1989 Alan Thompson this time caught Coal sub-sector locomotive 56135 *Port of Tyne Authority* leading MGR empties from Teesport to Ryhope Grange. The old housing has been cleared and the gasholders screwed down to an environmentally acceptable height; the foreground wasteland is beginning to resemble a jungle. *Both ART*

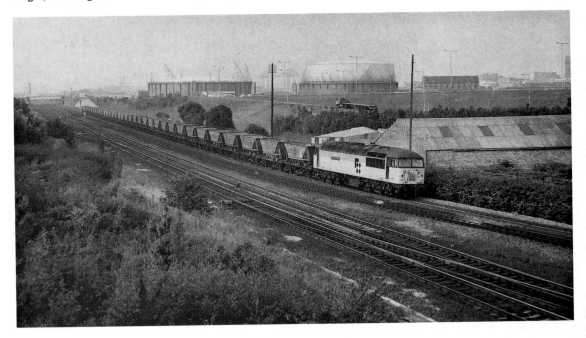

MIDDLESBROUGH GOODS: The transporter bridge looms larger as we approach Middlesbrough with this photograph found in John Armstrong's collection captioned simply 'North Eastern Railway Class "P" 0-6-0 No 1860 propelling the special train conveying the contents of Captain Cook's cottage into the goods yard'. We believe that this print was originally a press picture and further investigations seem to indicate that the cottage was shipped abroad 'lock, stock and barrel'. *JWA Collection*

The same junction today sees Thornaby's No 37518 leading a Lackenby-Wolverhampton Steel Terminal load around the curve into the straight leading to Newport and Thornaby. The Goods Terminal today principally handles potash rail/road interchange; the adjacent Dawson Transportation have leased a large area from BR and have their own '08' shunters. *ART*

MIDDLESBROUGH STATION GOODS DOCK (1): Looking from the Goods Dock back towards Thornaby, Class 'WD' No 90503 attacks the section up towards the Docks with empty steel-carrying vehicles in August 1965. *ART*

In November 1991 lineside bushes hide the view over the old town part of Middlesbrough and the Dock sidings are used by 'Pacer' units resting between turns. *KG*

MIDDLESBROUGH STATION GOODS DOCK (2): A short but interesting period in the evolution of BR's diesel traction fleet was the deployment of Class '14s' and '17s', and many of the latter came to the North. Looking in the opposite direction from the previous picture, we see one of the latter class on a typical short-haul trip duty, the sort of turns that are seen less and less today and, when found, are more usually in the hands of the cascaded-down Class '20s' or '31s'. It is May 1967 and Clayton No D8588 leads a string of 'salt' highfits from the Docks back to Haverton Hill and Tees Yard for redistribution. The classification of '9' may be correct, but the Southern Region destination ('0') is definitely fiction! A giveaway for a local trip engine, probably in hurried 'bonus-turn' working, is the 'toothpick' (shunting pole) seen on the side solebar of the engine. Above the rear wagons can be seen the pinnacle of the tiny Sussex Street gate box roof, pictured overleaf. In fact, this view affords a glimpse of three out of the four signal boxes in the immediate station area. *ART*

In May 1991 the demise of many of the businesses adjacent to the rails, with the distinct exception of the Troldahl Service Centre, confirms that in the intervening years this old town side of Middlesbrough has gone into decline. The Class '17s' slipped ignominiously from the North East scene in the early 1970s; '37s', '60s' (on freight) and 'Pacer' '153s' and '156s' on the local lines are the regulars of 1991. Only West cabin (now without the 'West') remains today to regulate traffic safely. *KG*

MIDDLESBROUGH STATION, WEST END (SUSSEX STREET): The driver of Class 'J26' No 65735 watches with professional interest as Class 'B16' No 61478 thuds over the Sussex Street roadway with an early '50s 'blood and spilt milk'-liveried trainset. The conical-shaped lead roof of the Sussex Street 'doll's-house' cabin only just accommodates the regulation-sized nameplate which it seems slightly perverse to have adhered to! The crossing, as may be imagined across such a busy 'throat' as this, could be a source of delay to both train and road traffic but was generally only used by road vehicles with high loads unable to go beneath the other bridges at either end of Middlesbrough station. *K. Hoole Collection*

Roads constructed over the railway effectively released this part of the town from being rail-locked, and thus Sussex Street went. The changes today are interesting, and we have included a wider aspect view to demonstrate how what was once the gate at the left-hand side is now fencing; the opposite side is a stone wall, but almost lost behind a plethora of poles. The former centre gatepost is now the site of Middlesbrough 676 signal and staff are asked to 'cross only when light shows'. *KG*

Middlesbrough was 'discovered' by the proprietors of the Stockton & Darlington Railway in 1826 whilst searching for a spot on the Tees with suitable depth to concentrate coal shipments, thus eradicating the double-handling required at Stockton, higher up the Tees. The location was occupied by a farm - Middlesbrough Farm - which was itself on the site of a Benedictine Monastic Church.

The first coals were shipped from this new staith in 1830 but the real action began in 1841 when Henry Bolckow and John Vaughan established their ironworks here and went from strength to strength after 1850 following the fortunate discovery of ironstone first in the Eston Hills then in other nearby locations. During the 40 years between 1873 and 1913 the Cleveland area produced an average of over five million tons of iron ore annually. At their zenith the mines supplied one-third of all Britain's requirements.

It is not difficult to see why the area required a comprehensive transport system. The river as a means of transport proved too shallow without navigable tributaries and consequently hastened along the development of railways whilst a canal was still under consideration. The network of lines to link the ironstone mines with the river-based blast furnaces quickly developed, the branch to Guisborough being the first, soon followed by the Cleveland Railway.

During the 1860s furnaces were opened away from central Middlesbrough, in places such as Normanby, Cargo Fleet, Newport and Linthorpe; by 1865 there were 12 ironworks in Stockton. Manufacturing iron for railway needs throughout the world meant a boom whilst materials for the North East's developing iron and steel shipbuilding phase resulted in an ever-present demand upon Tees-side's resources.

The latter years of the last century saw the start of the decline in the Cleveland iron industry and local steelmakers concentrated on fewer products of increased quality to keep a share of the world market. Diversification through developments on the northern Tees shore assured work for most, and the 1918 Ministry of Munitions ammonia site at Billingham has grown via steerage by Brunner Mond into the huge complex now known as ICI Billingham.

On the south side of the river (once the Yorkshire shore, but Cleveland since April 1974) modernisation and redevelopment has continued in spite of the end of ironstone mining at North Skelton in 1964. The existing Cleveland and Redcar works were integrated at a new site at Lackenby so that the processes involving preparation of ore, iron-making and coking could be concentrated at one site, steel making and rolling becoming specific to Lackenby.

Old Man Tees continues to play an important role in the local industrial scene, with imports of foreign ore and a planned influx of European coal perhaps giving the Coal Sector of Railfreight a greater involvement in Cleveland to balance against the dramatic decline of Durham's mining industry.

The area Metals Sector locomotive fleet based on Thornaby depot being now able to handle the heaviest hauls with new-generation Class '60s', it only leaves the passenger business hoping to switch into the electrification benefits enjoyed by towns along the East Coast Main Line. A glimmer of hope must exist in this direction and, together with the much talked about Cleveland Light Urban Railway, all these things should see Middlesbrough once again playing a key role in 21st-century transport developments.

MIDDLESBROUGH STATION, EXTERIOR (1): The station opened on 3 October 1877, 47 years after the Stockton & Darlington branched out from its historic first route. In the first photograph it is 1890. The road to the right is Exchange Place, whilst passing along the face of the station is Zetland Road. Although not a high-quality print, it certainly reflects the feel of this still new and burgeoning town when iron shipbuilding would seemingly go on for ever and 'steel' would never catch-on! (Fortunately the chemical industry was around the next industrial corner.) *Middlesbrough Library Collection, Cleveland County Council*

Eighty years on, by 1970 the iron trade has been and gone, and only the scars on the Cleveland hills testify to the great age of the ironmasters. In the station vaults Winterschladen had established his wine business that was to supply Kings and Queens at home and abroad, but is now in the descendancy. A 'P'-reg Rover 3500 and an Austin Cambridge make up the traffic as a tramp hopes he's found something valuable. The station profile is much altered as a result of war damage, and the Zetland House office block has risen up beyond. *BR*

By 1992 (*above*) the traffic has resulted in immense changes in the new town (south) side of the railway. The upper storey construction, seen in the last picture, proved to be temporary; the now revitalised station forecourt and buildings look full of new hope for a town hoping for 'City Partnership' honours under Langbaurgh Council leadership. A plaque on the wall next to the BR side entrance to the station (*right*) tells the story of Mr Winterschladen's achievements now that his business is only a memory. *Both KG*

Left MIDDLESBROUGH STATION, EXTERIOR (2): The parking area, seen in 1970, shows the original 1877 face incorporating the date stone. The religious overtones, typical of stations of this period, contrast strongly with the simplistic modern lines of Zetland House, lower down. *BR*

The 1992 comparison shows the recently refurbished and redesigned stone and roadwork. Although more pleasant it seems to have been designed to restrict taxi mobility and bollard damage is already getting to be repetitive. *KG*

Above MIDDLESBROUGH STATION (1): Not a pretty sight - this was the violent end of Middlesbrough's original overall roof, which was once regarded as a showpiece of architecture. The use of fine iron latticework incorporated within a gentle curve to culminate in a rather grand lantern apex made it conspicuous, and at the time it acted as publicity for the then state-of-the-art work of the ironmasters. The unlucky 'V' tank was of a type only recently transferred from Blaydon for work on the difficult Newcastle expresses. It seems that the sudden escape of steam from the blown-off cylinder head has resulted in a white steam-burn area, and the front pony truck is completely exposed. Goodness knows where the buffers went! The inscription on the picture is interesting as it reveals the careful censoring of pictures in wartime. Taken by the local *Middlesbrough Evening Gazette*, it was sent to the Information Agent of the LNER (then at King's Cross station) to be passed for publication in the newspaper. It was subsequently returned to the *Gazette* Editor endorsed 'Passed by censor but date MUST NOT be shown'. We can now reveal the date - 3 August 1942!

The station area was patched up as seen overleaf, but the remains hardly publicised the label 'iron capital of the North East'. The surviving roof section remained until a decision to remove it completely was made in early 1954. The subsequent tidying operations resulted in quite a poor rail-side 'greeting' for travellers to a town of this eminence! *BR*

MIDDLESBROUGH STATION (2): In this *circa* 1949 photograph, looking east, it can be seen that the station was hard pushed for 'through' platform occupancy with the result that the speed with which passengers were assisted on their way could sometimes be classed as unceremonious. . .! At peak holiday times an annex platform, to the west and accessed from Suffolk Place, was used for overspill services and a display board would be wheeled out pointing those for the east over to the 'Bridge Street Platform' (incidentally also the site of the fourth Middlesbrough station). *JWA*

The tower of the old parcels handling block at the far right-hand side, damaged by bombing, was eventually cleared and replaced by a modern brick structure in 1960. Called Zetland House, the majority of the offices were originally occupied by the not inconsiderable passenger and freight Commercial Manager's organisation for Teesside. Today it houses the Metals Sector control and management team for the Tees-Tyne (North East) freight area under the guidance of Mr Peter Mountain. The awning and the cast iron pillars below Zetland House remain as 'railway side' relics of post-war splendour. Flower beds help to brighten an otherwise functional look. *KG*

MIDDLESBROUGH STATION, EAST END (1): This August 1962 view from the other end of the station shows Thornaby Class 'V2' No 60901 hauling a limited stop excursion for Saltburn through platform 2 in the twilight years of mass excursionist traffic to the Yorkshire coastal resorts. To the right, passengers stand back to await the local 'stopper' for the Whitby and Saltburn lines. *K. Linford*

Twenty years on, the centre-piece signal and its 'dolly' have gone. So too has the middle road, now replaced by location boxes and watering points for today's units. The traditional 'add-to' brick huts to the left have been rationalised and a recently constructed rockery garden complements the remaining NER lattice support 'blooms' below the station awning. The platform has now been extended towards a station car-park access path. *KG*

MIDDLESBROUGH STATION, EAST END (2): Just out of works, Class 'L1' No 67754 looks well loaded with a healthy number of mid-morning passengers bound for Nunthorpe and Guisborough in the east-end bay. Alongside is Class 'A8' 4-6-2T No 69877 of Leeds Neville Hill standing on the short shunt neck at the head of parcels vans. The photograph also features Dock Hill signal cabin. *Ian Heyes Collection*

The current view includes a redundant platform face and roofing and reveals the elaborately finished building, the gable of which is just visible above the 'A8' - but of Dock Hill cabin there is no trace. *KG*

MIDDLESBROUGH STATION, EAST END (3): On 2 November 1969 D6777 is seen arriving from South Bank Iron Works with its shipment payload. The bay platform, then still used, contrasts with the rusty adjacent siding, and the non-standard Dock Hill cabin is prominent. *John Boyes*

In a typical comment upon the changing face of the North East, the March 1991 horizon has been scythed of dockland dinosaurs and a large tree envelopes the old junction site. The eastbound bay has returned to the mercy of nature, its day done. The decline of the docks here has been matched by the growth of deeper-draught berths at Teesport and the Redcar area; just as the S&D transferred operations from Stockton to Middlesbrough in 1830, the Eastern Region had no other choice but to move on again 150 years later. The common remaining items are the ornamental gable end on the left and, low in shrubbery, the signal box outbuilding (now with flattened roof). *KG*

MIDDLESBROUGH STATION, EAST END (4): Stepping back to a previous motive power era, this photograph was taken at a time when ex-LMS Ivatt 2-6-0s had become commonplace amongst the diminishing ranks of ex-NER mineral engines. It is late 1966 and No 43070 is an engine with a mission as it lifts the Thornaby re-railing tool-van trainset through the back road behind Middlesbrough station. It is correctly described by the lamps as a Class '1' express - going to 'clear the line'. Middlesbrough East signal box is seen at the end of the platform whilst a 'Q6' awaits the 'board' on the slow line. *ART*

Three years on, 2 November 1969, brings us to a steam-free railway. Viewed in close detail is Dock Hill, the junction with Middlesbrough Dock's railway complex. In contrast to the earlier view the dockland cranes are active and, on the left, D6777 (seen on the previous page) is now propelling its load of steel girders into the docks for shipment. By a coincidence the Thornaby tool-vans are again out and are about to return to the depot after re-railing vehicles in the dock area. In the interim, the LNER travelling crane has been replaced by a more modern version from the Cowans Sheldon Works at Carlisle, but the ex-TPO is still retained in the formation. *John Boyes*

According to the writings of the late Ken Hoole, **Middlesbrough shed** was first mentioned back in the mid-1840s; various primitive engine sheds subsequently went through the usual metamorphosis until by the 1860s it is known that a circular shed, with S&D origins, became redundant when construction began on what became a trio of large circular sheds clustered in a group, and interlinked, adjacent to Blake Street. The earlier shed had finally gone by 1877 to make way for the new, more central Middlesbrough station and thus the topography here settled down for the next 60 years.

Enforced changes came when, in January 1936, the roof of the coal stage collapsed in a gale and, four years later, the trio of sheds made an easy target for German bombers and the most westerly of the group, nearest to Blake Street, was flattened. Thereafter this roundhouse became well-known for giving photographers additional background views of the various funnel colours of the shipping companies using the docks!

From the 1880s Middlesbrough shed shared freight work with the emergent Newport installation but retained a passenger link. In this category were the tightly timed expresses over the difficult coastal route to Newcastle. Many experiments were made to find the perfect traction, and so it was, in late 1938, that the Class 'V' 2-6-2 tank engines proved to be the masters of the route. For this purpose Middlesbrough took five of the class from Blaydon on Tyneside in exchange for the same number of 'A8s', and the 2-6-2s became a feature from then until their demise.

However, the main activity at 51D remained freight operations. By the mid-1950s the area's maintenance logistics became costly. The answer proved to be at the area west of the old Newport shed near the old Erasmus Yards. The new depot became Thornaby and, by June 1958, took over the combined fleet from both the old inefficient sheds. The Blake Street area changed soon afterwards and today's views show that few tangible remaining features survive.

MIDDLESBROUGH MPD (1): *Below* The last day at Middlesbrough, 8 June 1958, showing the sorry state of the central round shed with the recently part demolished (and repaired) boiler house. Class 'Q6' No 63375 is prominent. *F. W. Hampson*

Right Today two Steam Age buffer-stops upon what appears to be truncated shed lines await their fate whilst the Docks, secured by Edward Pease with his 'Middlesbrough Owners' consortium, continue to serve a useful role. *KG*

MIDDLESBROUGH MPD (2): The middle of the roundhouse trio as seen in about 1953. By now ex-LMS design 'Mogul' 4MTs have infiltrated among the ex-NER types still predominant. Two Class 'V' tanks, Nos 67663 and 67685, are seen, together with Class 'Q6' No 63340 and 'G5' No 67281 (all with 51D shedplates). *Ian Heyes Collection*

The equivalent view today in what must be assumed to be the nearest position, but which was hampered by the motorway fencing. *KG*

MIDDLESBROUGH MPD (3): Another view of the last day, 8 June 1958, and Bill Hampson has caught the mood vividly. We look over the flattened remains of the bomb-damaged roundhouse and, to the right, the repaired roof of the coaling plant. The desolate ranks of NER workhorses await ferrying over to Thornaby where, we think you will agree, they did not look as much at home! *F. W. Hampson*

The approximate position today shows how Blake Street was swallowed up by urban motorway; remaining bits of BR property in this old shed area are utilised for plant storage by the Engineer. *KG*

CARGO FLEET: Both the Darlington-Middlesbrough-Saltburn branch and little Cargo Fleet station opened in 1846. Known then as Cleveland Port, the station was renamed in August 1867, and by 1911 it is recorded as taking the receipts of 55,000 passenger bookings annually! A high proportion were workers for the then thriving adjacent iron and steel works, known simply as 'Cochranes Works'. The station was dwarfed by the water-tower landmark of the Works, there to supply the once ever-active fleet of private motive power. Caught by John Boyes during 'elevenses' were, at the left-hand side of the upper picture, Hawthorn-Leslie 0-4-0ST *Cleveland* (Works No 2729/07) and, on the right-hand side and in the picture below, Hawthorn-Leslie 0-4-0ST *Cochranes No 6* (Works No 3481/20). *John Boyes*

Along with so much of the traditional heavy engineering firms along the banks of the Tees, it is sad to relate that the demise of the Works in the late '70s resulted in the closure of the station in 1989. The 1990 view (*above*) shows the platforms still extant but awaiting trimming bank. W. G. Beadman Ltd now occupies a corner of the once rambling Works site. The little tank engines died in the blast furnaces . . . presumably in very small pieces. *ART*

CARGO FLEET BSC WORKS: On 5 August 1969 BR began a daily transfer of molten metal from Cargo Fleet Works to Consett Iron Works in order to maintain production at the latter whilst several blast furnaces were being rebuilt. Three specially-designed 'torpedo' wagons to contain the metal at 1,600^{0}C were made available for the starting day, illustrated here. It was the first occasion that molten metal had travelled more than 5 miles on BR on a regular basis. Train '6X93' is seen shortly before departure with the 12.30 service to Consett led by two Class '37' engines, then numbered 6791 and 6712. The trains ran via Stillington, Tursdale Junction, Leamside, Felling and Tyne Yard to gain access to the Consett bank at Ouston Junction. Their maximum speed was no higher than 20 mph. In view of the immense financial outlay involved, one wonders whether the BSC had hoped to extend further the life of Consett beyond the immediate reshaping of British Steel. *John Boyes*

All is conjecture now, as it can be seen that not only was Consett Iron Works razed but also its temporary life-line at Cargo Fleet. On 26 March 1990 a Class '47' passes the flattened site with a tank train from ICI Wilton. The lineside pathway known as the 'Sailors Trod' has subsequently been diverted here and a new road is in the course of construction. *ART*

NUNTHORPE: Once in the rural heartland, the tentacles of industrial Cleveland have gradually crept nearer Nunthorpe until today it serves many thousands as compared to the hamlet of 1900 recorded as having only 198 people. The line came this way in 1853 to connect Tees-side with the ore-rich hinterland running in the general direction of Guisborough, and the mines owned by the railway-connected Pease family. The station opened the following year, soon to become the junction station for the Whitby line off to the south. Our 1950 picture illustrates a Class 'G5'-hauled push-pull train eking out the final months of service on the Guisborough branch. Even this minimum train-set was unable to keep the line in the black. *JWA*

Today's station sees a peak-time shuttle to Middlesbrough with four Whitby line trains each way. We show 'Pacer' No 142083 arriving on 27 July 1989 with a midday Whitby-Middlesbrough service. The signal box is the last along the branch, the remaining miles to Whitby being signalled on the 'no block' principle and Nunthorpe acting as the command post for three intermediate token exchange points *en route*. The 'Pacer' has just come off the single-line section and will now continue on double track to Middlesbrough. 1992 will see the planned introduction of single-unit Class '153s' with a cab at each end, and surely this ultimate in economy will make even the 'G5' auto-train look labour-intensive! *ART*

GUISBOROUGH: The mentor of the Guisborough branch enterprise was Joseph Pease who used his powers of persuasion to build towards his ironstone mines in this district, thus forming the Middlesbrough & Guisborough Railway Co. The branch of approximately 10 miles was opened to goods traffic by November 1853, making way for the passenger service to begin the following February, worked by and eventually taken over completely by the S&D. By 1878 came the link to the east via the rival Cleveland Railway, but Guisborough remained a dead-end station on a through route and was consequently an obvious choice for push-pull working. Following the demise of the BTP sets in 1929, railcars in 1941 and then the push-pull-fitted 'G5s' in 1954, the branch saw its final operations performed by 'A8' and 'V' tanks. In this *circa* 1960 photograph we see Class 'V' No 67640 awaiting return to Middlesbrough with excursion stock. *K. Linford*

In March 1990 the only remaining reference points are the many-chimneyed houses formerly to be seen above the station name-sign. The station closed completely in August 1964 and a man on a ladder has replaced No 67640! *ART*

Cleveland coast

This is an auspicious time for **Redcar** for, as can be seen from our 'present' views below and overleaf, much has happened to alter the general arrangement of the passage of trains in the eastbound direction. Of even greater importance, however, is the carefully executed restoration work on the body of the station buildings, not only to breathe new life into this fine listed Victorian structure but also to restore mainstream activity into a once fading part of a growing township.

The work, overseen by BR's Project Manager George Hodgson (pictured below), was paid for by the now popular and successful 'partnership' concept whereby BR's Community Unit enters into agreement with the Local Authority, in this case Langbaurgh, to share the costs of a revitalisation scheme involving BR property being put to useful modern community use, allied (naturally) to convenient transport benefits. It is a simple concept without any catches, and has recently brought many bouquets to BR.

The result of this forward thinking in the case of Redcar is a sight for sore eyes for all those who appreciate classic architectural style vis-à-vis useful old stations! None the less, one laments that BR's Community Unit was so late acoming; we can only conjecture what such a partnership scheme could have meant to such places as the Manors district of Newcastle (currently part of a Science Park Development, but now without the 'heritage' site buildings), or to Stockton's once proud train-shed.

REDCAR (1): *Below left* BR's Project Manager George Hodgson beside the board advertising the Redcar Station Business Centre Phase I - 'A Partnership in Enterprise'.

Below right A view of the interior work with the rail pit awaiting infilling as part of Phase II. All damaged woodwork and doors were reconstructed using original plans, and York stone was brought in to replace that damaged during the years of neglect. The half-dozen work units will enjoy the best of materials, past and present! When completed, Redcar seems destined to become a classic example of how BR can influence a greater sphere than just the immediate railway. *Both KG*

REDCAR (1): The first photograph shows a typical day in October 1964 when Metro-Cammell DMUs still ruled supreme. We are standing at the Middlesbrough end of the platform with a Saltburn-bound service about to restart towards the road crossing. A chilly wind has everyone in winter garb and Transit Coaches have been quick to usurp the NER presence at the warehouse. *JWA Trust*

In order to incorporate the train-shed within the revival plans, the eastbound line was slewed across to run behind the train-shed wall and a new temporary platform erected alongside. Phase I of the scheme is shown in the centre and lower views nearing completion in early 1991. *Both KG*

REDCAR EXCURSION PLATFORM: This is the only view we discovered of this once wide spread of platform built to meet the needs of excursions and the (still) popular racecourse activities, but now forgotten and derelict. The main station lies beyond in this old view, and what looks like a railway 'bobby' stands awaiting to preserve some semblance of order with a special due! Dated to the turn of the century, it may be a surprise to readers that the photograph shows the platforms so overgrown. This surely dents the lovingly held perceptions of a scrupulous NER! *JWA Trust Collection*

It was impossible to repeat the same view because of construction work, but the second (1964) view perhaps supplies a part answer to the weeds puzzle, for it indicates that the platform area around the ticket booth was simply flattened soil. *JWA*

MARSKE: On the Darlington-Middlesbrough-Saltburn branch of 1861, Marske lost its goods loading facilities in November 1963, and, as can be seen in this 1956 photograph, milk churns seem to have played a prominent role in receipts! The station buildings are distinctive if only from the point of view of the heavy barge-boarding with signal-type finials incorporated at the apex. *JWA*

Marske today still does brisk business with the bucket-and-spade brigade but is also a desirable dormitory town for the workers of Cleveland. The Perspex-windowed bus-style shelter that replaced the steep-roofed buildings was photographed from a passing Saltburn service in November 1991. Some old fencing has survived for a fresh coat of paint and, together with the platform, still ends at the bridge parapet beyond. *KG*

NEAR MARSKE: By 1963 only the occasional services on the Saltburn line were still in the hands of steam. The majority of trains to and from Darlington were DMUs and ran two-hourly with an injection of services to and from Stockton at workers' peak times. One such extra was the 17.09 (SX) from Stockton which, to Alan Thompson's disgust, was always seen running bunker-first on its outward run. This photo is therefore a rarity, and the result of a chase through busy homebound traffic to beat the '4MT' to this position.

The Class '143' 'Pacer' sets of the late '80s were soon to give way to '142s' and 'Sprinters' on the long Bishop Auckland-Saltburn run when Alan Thompson returned in March 1990 and inadvertently recorded the demise of another traction form! Here No 143604 sweeps below the same overbridge, now with its Steam Age soot layers dropping off to reveal clean sandstone beneath. *Both ART*

Saltburn-by-the-Sea was one of the first seaside towns to be created by the advent of railways, and credit for the initiative must go once more to Darlington Quaker, iron-master and Stockton & Darlington entrepreneur Henry Pease. He saw that an extension of the railway from Redcar would not only build up patronage of the Saltburn area but would also facilitate better services to his mines at Skelton. The Saltburn Improvement Commission resulted and George Dickinson of Darlington was asked to plan a new town extension around the station. Thomas Prosser is thought to have been the station architect and its general appearance fitted in well with the architecture of the other houses around the station square.

However, Pease was made aware by the Saltburn residents that no bawdy 'cheap-day-returners' would be tolerated, and although some did visit, petitions and 'other threats' resulted in NER Directors effectively discouraging the like from this genteel watering place! Eventually the residents had to capitulate on the class issue when, threatened by the expansion of Whitby, Scarborough and, more seriously, the Lancashire seaboard resorts, the town entered the fray to attract anyone and everyone, thenceforth easily balancing the books. Between 1877 and 1911 an incredible 114,236 journeys were made annually *from* the resort; one wonders what the arrivals figure must have been!

Landmarks associated with those far-off Victorian crowds tend to have been destroyed since the mid-1970s (the Ha'penny Slide and the Valley Gardens fun railway, for example). But even though there may have been a time when Saltburn was not proud of its past, the same cannot be said today, thanks to the enterprise of the Council. The station area is again a focal point, and whilst the town continues in its role as a genteel residential area, there is also a place for the workers of Tees-side, and the promotion of its Victorian heritage.

Associated with the excursion peak of the 1930s are the LNER posters which vividly portrayed the character of the Yorkshire Coast. These were truly the 'Glorious Years' for railways and it is no overstatement to say that only now has the tide begun to turn towards a new railway era. As with Redcar, Saltburn today shows the hand of cooperation between the Community, Council and BR, as roads become less adequate.

SALTBURN (1): The old station facade at Saltburn is one of the finest pieces of Victoriana in the north. It brings to mind the style of the Grand Junction Railway architecture, and has a hint of the lost Doric arch at Euston. Today the traveller bypasses the old entrance to reach the trains (on the left of the photograph) or can shop or eat at the premises that have replaced the station staff offices. *KG*

SALTBURN (2): Here is the station in the 1963 'limbo' period when PSO grants were just a twinkling in the accountants' eye and provincial railways everywhere were searching for a new direction. *JWA*

The same setting today, although unstaffed and basic, shows the clean lines of the station's platform furniture, and a convenient user-friendly timetable catches the eye of passing shoppers. (The bay on the right has since lost its rails.) *KG*

The Zetland Hotel was planned as the prestige development associated with Pease's plans for the town. Designed by William Peachey (remembered more for his Manchester Central creation, now the G-Mex site), the hotel opened on 27 July 1863 at a cost of £12,000 with an additional outlay of £5,000 for the furniture! Its popularity fluctuated like the weather in these parts and it is said that the first manager was removed from duty due to certain 'irregularities' down in the wine cellar. By 1877, the economic slump had almost forced its closure.

   The most convenient station-to-hotel facility perhaps anywhere in Britain was designed by an NER with sights upon the upper-middle-class clientele. Once at the Zetland Hotel, arriving passengers were met by smart uniformed hotel porters and ushered into the hushed luxury of the hotel reception. The Zetland offered early en suite facilities and an unrivalled coastal view - it quickly gained in popularity, becoming the place to be seen! Although twice 'let', it remained under railway ownership, staying with BR up until 1975. It is used now as flats.

SALTBURN (3): The first of the three views shows the hotel end of the main platform in the late '50s when rails ran up to the buffer-stop, although engines were no longer allowed under the awning as a coal cell was provided at the head-shunt. *JWA*

   The second view was taken by BR to record the pre-sale situation in 1974. *BR*

   By 1991 (*above*) the small hotel warehouse (once the stables and coach-house for the wealthy) has given way to parking spaces for flat-owners, and a small flight of steps gives access to the platform, which is barred in two places; the fence shown precludes access to the Zetland Flats from the old people's homes. Behind the photographer the platform profile continues all the way to the current station, but includes private walkways. *KG*

SALTBURN (4): The similarities between this view of the train-shed and hotel beyond and that of the train-shed at Redcar undergoing restoration (page 47) are striking. Also striking is the 1960s 'Monica' 'See a friend this weekend' advertisement that has gone down in railway poster lore! *JWA*

The view along the platform from the current buffer-stops towards the Zetland Hotel shows that the old platform is now a 'shoppers' platform' with access to shops, cafes and tourist agencies that today occupy what were, up until the late 1960s, the boarded-up offices of ex-NER staff. The shops are imaginatively named to link with the railway theme in a way that gently acknowledges all that the town owes to the coming of the iron horse. *KG*

SALTBURN MPD: Until 1863 Saltburn's source of readily available motive power was at Redcar, but because of many complaints of passenger train delays due to locomotives arriving '. . . too early and late', the engine shed was resited at Saltburn. Here the original 1864 two-engine shed and its associated venerable water tank are seen, and behind Class 'V2' No 60968 is the four-engine extension of 1877. This picture, dating from 29 July 1958, was taken six months after the shed had closed and its band of six Class 'A8s' had been placed into lengthy storage, eventually to be withdrawn, the victims of early dieselisation on the route. The depot continued as a holding area for incoming steam-hauled excursions (as shown here) into the mid-'60s. *JWA Trust Collection*

The May 1989 view shows the still standing but closed goods depot to the right of the now cleared shed site. The line to Boulby skirts the right-hand side of the view, and a Darlington-bound 'Pacer' unit is seen. *KG*

HUNT CLIFF, BROTTON: The twisting summit gradient of the line here, lashed by north-easterly squalls, has put paid to the progress of many a train! In 1963, in clement conditions, Class 'Q6' No 63431 of Tyne Dock (52H) and recently outshipped from Darlington made a good choice for an SLS railtour over these freight-only lines in 1963. A considerate crew have stopped to allow photographs at the cliff-edge location. No 63431 stayed a Tyne Dock engine until 1966, then transferring to West Hartlepool for its final months of activity. In August 1967 it went into storage until being towed back up the coast to North Blyth and the engine and shipbreaker's yard of Hughes Bolckow in September of that year. She was one of the last survivors of steam on the North East coast. K. Linford

58

The Saltburn-Whitby line closed in 1958, but then in 1970 Cleveland Potash approached BR for help in transporting thousands of tons of the alkaline substance along approximately 3 miles of the old route from Boulby mine. Reinstatement of the line was not without major engineering difficulties for BR, but by 1977 traffic was flowing once again on these high cliffs above the often angry North Sea. It was initially assumed that pairs of the versatile Class '31s' would ably negotiate the steep winding road out from the mine, but their high power-to-weight ratio (due to their central non-powered axle) proved their undoing and the Metals Sector eventually replaced them with Class '37/4' engines. The ideal engine, however, remained the ageing (1957-introduced) English Electric Type 1 Class '20s'. On 26 June 1989, and now on single track, Class '20' Nos 20118 *Saltburn-by-the-Sea* and 20165 *Henry Pease* stalk gingerly around the cliff edge running parallel to the Cleveland Coastal walkway prior to the Class '37' takeover. *ART*

CRAG HALL, SKINNINGROVE: With BSC exchange sidings still busy behind Crag Hall signal box, the route to the right had almost become unnecessary when the 1970 re-opening was proposed. Back in 1958 token exchange on/off the Whitby branch had recently ended as 'Q6' No 63430 (midway between transfer from the old Newport MPD (51B) and the new Thornaby depot) grapples with a train consisting mainly of nine-plank coke empties, and struggles over the tortuous ladder of points from the BSC area westward to Newport Yard. Withdrawn from Thornaby in April 1963, No 63430 was cut up at Darlington Works a month later. *JWA*

On the same day as the previous 'present' photograph, the same Class '20s' are seen passing the token cabin as they leave the Boulby branch with a loaded train to Middlesbrough Goods Terminal. Changes to note include the introduction of draught-proof windows to the signal cabin and the re-introduced token platform at a higher level. *ART*

Inset No 20118's nameplate, photographed at Thornaby TMD. *KG*

It is of interest to note that Boulby was Britain's first, and the world's deepest, potash mine with one shaft diving about 4,000 feet underground. The mine was first planned to be located at Hawsker but was altered due to logistics. First discovered in 1950, it had to wait until 1968 for deep-mining technology to catch up with events. Work began at Boulby on 16 April 1969. Incidentally, the Hawsker site may have led to eventual coastal passenger services again because by early 1970 BR had completed signalling schemes at Whitby Bog Hall to enable Hawsker potash trains to work into Whitby and run round there! But it was not to be.

NORTH YORKSHIRE

Leeds Northern

YARM: The 1852 Leeds Northern Railway Company's route between the Midland Railway junction at Leeds (Holbeck) and Stockton, via Yarm, may be thought of as an early railway work, but Yarm's claim to fame stretches back much further, in fact to the world-famous Stockton & Darlington Railway. Yarm was joined to the S&D by way of a coal depot, opened in October 1825, but was not included in the S&D 'main-line' service, having to await the construction of the LNR route seen here to gain a passenger link with the outside world. In 1954 a midday Newcastle to York express speeds past the enamel 'VIROL' signs on the LNR warehouse behind Gresley Class 'A3' No 60071 *Tranquil*. Behind, in the goods yard, stand four vans, each of a different diagram pattern, an indication of the rich variety of rolling-stock in that era. *JWA*

The passenger service having ceased early in 1960, and the goods facilities being withdrawn four years later, our May 1989 picture shows a freight-only branch denuded of station traces and being quickly bypassed by the mid-afternoon Haverton Hill-Parkeston (6L81) Speedlink service behind Class '47' No 47315. The tunnel at the rear of the train was dug beneath the 1825 route to the coal depots and today carries the Darlington-Yarm road. *ART*

The good news as we go to press is that Regional Railways North East have recognised the potential of the well-populated Yarm-Eaglescliffe corridor by not only giving residents a two-hourly fast train to the Midlands/North-West but also planning for a new Yarm Town station to be situated within easy town access. This not only reinforces BR's commitment to Tees-side growth but should also see housing developments spring up again along the old LNR main line.

Below The arches of the viaduct crossing the River Tees at Yarm frame the town's oldest remaining church whilst high above Class 'WD' No 90071 potters along with the now obsolete 'iron ore tipplers' forming the 14.15 Wensley-West Hartlepool ore train on 20 May 1965. *John Boyes*

YARM VIADUCT: A short way south of Yarm station, the Leeds Northern coastal route traverses the 43-arched Yarm Viaduct of 1849, bridging the low vale and town. Not so noticeable in our earlier, 1955, view are the fluctuations in the level of the viaduct at track level. The May 1989 picture, however, shows more clearly the need for the additional support arches to counter the effects of subsidence. Back in 1955, Class 'V2' No 60879 crosses the viaduct with through King's Cross-Sunderland carriages (3 pm from London), whilst the contemporary scene shows the line's traditional 'bread and butter' commodity - coal - in this case coal empties returning to the Durham pits from the Aire Valley power stations. The change of viewpoint was forced by the growth of the trees seen in the forefront of the earlier scene. *JWA/ART*

65

PICTON: At the junction of the Leeds Northern route to Battersby, Picton was once a busy 'regulating' point on this route, having a signal box capacity to boot, with, today, many 'spare' levers. In the early '50s a Northallerton 'Super-D' ('D20'), No 62347, is caught returning home with a pigeon van and a train of passenger stock. The signal box operates a fine pair of slotted-post signals, and has a large collection of fire-buckets at the ready! The 'up' side waiting room is glimpsed but has now gone. *JWA Trust Collection*

In today's view it can be seen that the signal box's bricked-up lower windows have dissolved into the scheme of things, the fire-buckets have gone (to collectors?) and the trailing connection into the goods shed area has been removed. It is now 30 May 1989 and No 56122 *Wilton Coalpower* storms up the grade taking Durham coal towards the cluster of power stations in the Aire Valley. *ART*

The additional view (*bottom*) supports the theory that time has slowed down here. The gatewheel, gates and station master's house provide a vignette not commonly found at operational locations today. *KG*

NORTHALLERTON, LEEDS NORTHERN: Continuing from the ECML coverage in 'Past and Present' No 11, we now look at the railway peripherals at the lower level of the Leeds Northern route from Melmerby to Stockton, begun by the Leeds & Thirsk company. Our first pictures are viewed from the ECML upper level and look north-east towards the Low Gates direction where the LN built its first station. By 1856 the curve joining the LN to the York, Newcastle & Berwick (on the right) came into commission, so that this LN station became obsolete when interchange could be achieved under one roof, that of the present station. A low level platform subsequently followed, over to the south-west, and from 1901, by utilising a new connection on the ECML, services from Melmerby could use either the high or low level stations and thus both routes. On 25 June 1966, EE Type 4 (Class '40') No D275 brings a Newcastle-Colchester (via Sunderland) train up the LN route over Springwell Lane crossing and under the ECML route on the approach to Northallerton (Low Level). This service evidently did not call at Northallerton or it would have taken the spur to the right that led into the main High Level station. D275 will join the ECML on the up side at Longlands Junction after weaving a figure 'S'.

On 28 February 1992 the neat row of railway-inspired houses looks just as trim, but a new generation of Cortinas and Minis has replaced the '60s scrap pile of Commer, Bedford and Albion lorries, vans and ambulances. Springwell Lane crossing leading into the scrapyard now has its full complement of warning signs and flashing lights, whilst a Metals Sector Class '37' takes a light RFD consignment north over the LN route towards Tees Yard from Crewe Basford Hall. *Both KG*

NORTHALLERTON, ROMANBY GATES: The northern extent of the Low Level station was physically curtailed by this busy road crossing called Romanby Gates. Caught in the mid-'50s is this Liverpool-Newcastle Sunday train required to take the LN route northbound due to an ECML total engineering possession. Class 'A3' No 60084 *Trigo* has brought a Bedford OB half-cab to a halt on the Ripon run, although no passengers seem delayed! *JWA*

The now familiar continental-style barriers with flashing lights have made the crossing box obsolete. It is now 29 June 1989 and Thornaby's dedicated Metals engines Nos 37506 *British Steel Skinningrove* and 37512 *Thornaby Demon* throttle up for the attack on Picton with the return empties of the Corby-Lackenby steel-liner service. The large building in the background is a County Council depot, now with a high radio mast. Nettles cover the site of the former cabin. *ART*

69

NORTHALLERTON LOW LEVEL: Class 'A3' No 60092 *Fairway* of Newcastle's Heaton shed departs southwards from the Low Level station with another diverted Sunday express in the early 1950s. These Second World War emergency-use platforms were retained for some time after hostilities ceased for just such a contingency as illustrated, for the ECML was constantly being realigned and upgraded as more money became available to the BTC to restore pre-war line speeds. The little Northallerton depot is seen on the right with most of its allocation dotted around, whilst the signal bracket features an interesting combination of colour light displays at the base of the main semaphore. The lights were required on this last semaphore signal to introduce the correct aspect sequence when 'striking in' to the then all-new colour-light-signalled ECML. *JWA*

By 17 March 1992 the tidy hedge once bordering the Council building to the left has sprung up in wild abandon as North East Coal Sector engine No 56132 treads carefully past the platform site with 1,500 tons of Durham coal for the south. The shed's replacement building grew up in the late 1960s, and provides a stark contrast to the ornate Victorian stonework. *ART*

NORTHALLERTON MPD (1): The shed in detail as seen in the early '50s with two regular Northallerton engines, Nos 62388 ('D20') and 62044 ('K1') facing south. Adjacent on the right and only just seen is the water tank and the Shed Master's office with a non-standard porch roof against the backdrop of the main upper level ECML station roofing.

The other view was taken in about 1970 when the shed site, although cleared, still showed some truncated connections. The shed, closed by March 1963 and demolished in November 1964, has been replaced by Bibby's agricultural food factory, which is still active. The station roof and back wall of the main station are the same, but it appears that JWA's lens is out of alignment with a slight loss of definition. *Both JWA*

NORTHALLERTON MPD (2): With the old diagonal fencing in the foreground, John took this view from the main-line station looking down over the shed sprawl and both LN Low Level platforms beyond. Class 'J73' No 68359 is parked with some NER wooden 'high' wagons against the engineer's loading dock. *JWA*

At a slightly different angle due to intervening years of tree growth, the March 1992 view shows the dramatic change since Bibby's food factory replaced the shed. The factory looks to be well matured since the previous view (at construction time) was taken. The Council building's side-on extension looks as though it has always been there, although it would have impinged upon the Low Level down platform in earlier times. It is a sobering thought that the old steam shed which gave a livelihood to many Northallerton families is today hardly remembered by townspeople. *ART*

Picton to Battersby

PICTON: Looking southwards from the up side platform at Picton, it can be seen that Class 'G5' No 67343 has just come off the branch from Battersby via Stokesley, carrying the section token (the junction with its connections can be seen beyond). The leisurely pace is unmistakable, with an open-top tractor (Fordson?) and a bicycle waiting for the token hand-over ceremony to take place. *JWA*

Racing on 40 years to 1991, the old LN is on the threshold of a major turnaround in interest. When this volume appears Picton will be a key point in regulation again, not, however, with slow branch incursions but with a brand new Middlesbrough-Liverpool service needing to meld with the already heavy Train Load Freight presence. One example in this category is shown here, but with a questionable life. It is the British Steel-sponsored service from Redmire Quarry, seen heading towards Tees-side with approximately 1,800 tons of crushed limestone and hauled by two Thornaby Metals '37s'. The road has not narrowed over the years - the lower camera angle has foreshortened it! *ART*

POTTO: Driving slowly through the village a number of times, it was the signboard 'THE OLD STATION' which caught our attention along what is now just another meandering Yorkshire byway. The station is now occupied by a freelance artist, who was extremely interested to see the 'past' view and came outside to point out the remaining railway connections and alterations he had made or knew about.

It can be seen that the former waiting room area has been built up into a first floor corresponding to the main frontage, giving a respectably sized property. A rockery and shrub garden stand where once did Class 'G5' No 67343 on a Whitby-Stockton service back on 1951, and the riders of tandems would experience fewer delays at the crossing gates after 1954 for, as the accompanying poster (*right*) tells us, the 1857 line was not to see its centenary, at least as a passenger route. On Monday 14 June 1954 passenger facilities were withdrawn, and Ingleby (page 80) was closed entirely. *JWA/KG/JWA*

While taking the 'present' pictures, it was discovered that in the area on the other side of the crossing the opposite side platform was very much in evidence, but a remarkable find was this early Pooley small consignments weighing machine (*below*); the owner of the station house intended to take it in when it was pointed out. It can be seen that the surrounding forest was closing in, and this artefact was completely hidden in summertime. *KG*

BRITISH RAILWAYS

WITHDRAWAL OF PASSENGER TRAIN SERVICE

The British Transport Commission announce that on and from Monday 14th June the passenger train service will be withdrawn from the following stations :—

TRENHOLME BAR	STOKESLEY
POTTO	INGLEBY
SEXHOW	

ALTERNATIVE ROAD SERVICES

Alternative road services for passengers are provided by the following operators :—
UNITED AUTOMOBILE SERVICES LTD.
CROWE BROS.
DUNNINGS GREEN LINE

PARCELS

The collection and delivery of parcels will continue as at present.

FREIGHT TRAIN TRAFFIC

Freight train traffic in full loads will continue to be dealt with at all stations except Ingleby which will be closed entirely. Through loads of freight traffic for Ingleby will be handled at Battersby Station.

There will be no change in the method of dealing with freight traffic in less than full truck loads.

Any further information can be obtained from the District Commercial Superintendent, British Railways, Middlesbrough (Telephone 2821) or from any Station Master. If desired arrangements will be made for a representative to call.

SEXHOW: Midway along the 1857 North Yorkshire & Cleveland Railway route between Picton and Battersby stood the tiny rural station of Sexhow, catering for the adjacent neighbouring hamlets of Busby, Carlton-in-Cleveland, Faceby and Sexhow itself, 1 mile distant. The early view is of Class 'A8' No 69858 with a Whitby to Stockton stopping service. The narrowness of the sleepered road crossing perhaps indicates the pace of rural life at sleepy Sexhow. With only a small amount of stone traffic, the station relied heavily on passenger receipts, which by the early '50s could not even support the Station Master's wages. *JWA*

Closed before Beeching in June 1954, the only clue to the location was the aptly named and beautifully renovated station building almost completely hidden by shrubbery and called 'The Sleepers', the garden of which, covering the former platform area, was photographed in early 1989. *ART*

This page John Midcalf found it easy to find directions to the vanished station site in 1990, a mere 36 years after closure! At Hutton Rudby (*right*) the clock appears to have stopped in 1954 and the signpost still wishfully points to Sexhow Station, and proudly announces the 'North Riding' of Yorkshire in the circle above. *Both John Midcalf*

STOKESLEY: The next station along the branch towards Battersby, Stokesley served a potential travelling public of 2,716 people in 1911 and booked 16,514 rail journeys in that year. Our old view, from May 1954, shows a substantial station with goods facilities dealing mainly in hay and clover of a very definite rural character. The LNER public noticeboard on the signal box is still proudly displaying the old company name as Class 'G5' 0-4-4 No 67240 prepares to leave. It appears that the crew are keen for John to include them! *JWA*

Like the other stations along this line, Stokesley lost its passenger service on 14 June 1954, whilst the local farmers' goods service was severed in August 1965. We visited the location in January 1990, and this is what was found. We had heard that the signal box may have survived but were disappointed to discover no sign of it. It seemed sensible to enquire within the now tidily renovated Station House and surprise, surprise, as we stood at the enquiry desk in the reception area, there through the end window was the old cabin (*right*)! It was tucked in adjacent to a private dwelling facing the location that it had graced for so long. It was pleasing to see such a well-renovated cluster of station buildings and we gratefully acknowledge the firm of architects for granting us permission to look over the old place. *Both KG*

Our final view of Stokesley (*below right*) catches a quiet moment at about the turn of the century. The station has its full 'kit' of furnishings, garden accessories and a large goods warehouse. A figure can be seen dimly in the office on the left, but otherwise there is no sign of human life. *National Railway Museum, York*

INGLEBY: This 1951 photo by John Armstrong gives the illusion that the porter on the right is about to commit suicide! Fortunately it is nothing so dramatic, for the engine is propelling its train out of one platform to continue its journey on the other line (such was the operating contingency when the section towards Stokesley became singled due to wagon storage on the other track). *JWA*

Closed entirely when the branch service ended in June 1954, Ingleby today is worth a visit, with the down-side platform imaginatively incorporated within a two-tiered play lawn. More deception here today needs explaining: the spire-roofed building in the 'past' scene is not the same as that seen in the 'present' photograph. The owners have opened out the area once steeply roofed and added a first floor. Today we see the entire building. *KG*

BATTERSBY (1): The station opened in 1867, and Battersby became a 'railway town' in a similar mould to Riccarton, although *with* road access! Battersby Junction until 1893, after the Second World War it gradually depended slightly more on its passenger receipts than for its goods, in particular the ironstone from Rosedale (see pages 84ff). Looking south-westwards we see an unidentified Class 'A8' tank with a neat three-coach set reposing in the summer sun whilst the crew prepare to swing out the column bag. Further down, the signpost-style 'Trains For' board seems inappropriate where there can hardly be much confusion! It nevertheless must have been useful at one time when trains could arrive/depart in three directions and a bit of late running would have meant plat-forming problems. The signs survive but Battersby is now unstaffed on both station and signal box. *JWA*

Looking in the same direction but from the opposite side of the platform towards today's buffer-stops (the line on to Picton having long since closed), a 'Pacer' awaits departure time with a train from Whitby to Middlesbrough in November 1990. *KG*

BATTERSBY (2): The east (Whitby-facing) end of Battersby in June 1954 with Class 'B1' No 61034 *Chiru* at the head of a special train shortly before the Picton line closed later that month. A Middlesbrough-Whitby service awaits line clearance on the left, with the ironstone hills forming a backdrop behind some recently uplifted mineral roads. Millions of tons of ironstone must have passed this junction over the years, having come down the Ingleby Incline over the NER's Rosedale branch with produce from the mines at Blakey, Sheriffs, Hollins and the East Mines complex. As well as extensive sidings, Battersby also had a three-road engine-shed and turntable to cope with the traffic, and two terraces of 30 cottages to house those connected with the mines and railway. *JWA*

On 30 May 1989 it is still a location of great antiquity (semaphores, water column and classic signal box), and is the passing place of up and down direction 'Pacer' DMUs. The birch trees over to the right have grown quickly to obliterate the moorland view, and the ironstone traffic area has been replaced by muddy pools to afford car-parking spaces and sleeper storage (pending sale to farmers) for the Civil Engineer. *ART*

Shortly after the 1989 photograph was taken, S & T Engineers recovered a lorry-load of signals from Battersby when the line from Nunthorpe through to Whitby went over to 'no block' token signalling. In spite of this much of interest remains, centred around the NER-plated water-column and tank. In this November 1990 picture (*above*), a Whitby service departs; the driver had changed ends and operated the token release for the next section minutes before rain clouds blacked out the station. *KG*

Rosedale

This fascinating and long-dead rail system is still vigorously investigated by hoards of devotees who still seem to uncover new facts, mostly because the railway was generally allowed to 'weather away' naturally and many relics thus still remain.

Rosedale, a deep valley extending 8 miles from the North Yorkshire Moors watershed area with its lone village at Rosedale Abbey, today relies upon summer visitors for something of the old bustle it knew so long ago at the height of ore mining operations.

It was over 100 years ago that mining began in a modern industrial way when broad seams of very magnetic and high-quality ironstone were discovered by John Vaughan in the dale side 1 mile south of the Rosedale Abbey. (Incidentally, there was never an Abbey here, only a Nunnery.) During the early years of large-scale output the ore was taken by horse-drawn wagons to Pickering and thence carried by rail via Malton and Pilmoor bound for various ironworks, but frequently to the Consett Iron Company.

The NER had by 1861 completed a half-mile incline tramway to assist transportation, and the associated engine winding house resulted in the once familiar Yorkshire landmark known as Rosedale chimney, demolished in July 1972.

During the first 17 years (1860-1877) ore output was at its peak, but from 1877 - as seams narrowed - pits became less viable with closures beginning in 1879. Never the less the NER erected a substantial stone-built engine shed in 1861 and it continued in use right up to the last pit closures in 1926. Demolition followed in 1937-8.

The shed was sited near the head of the tramway incline linking Hollins Mine to the standard gauge railway leading across the plateau of the moors to Blakey (3^1/$_2$ miles away) and Ingleby. Built at a height of 970 feet above sea level, a small community of 16 cottages soon grew up alongside the engine shed. From our centrally-heated sitting-rooms we can only wonder at the deprivations of the enginemen who worked here through eight-month winters of 12-hour minimum shifts when the simple task of acquiring provisions was an expedition demanding many miles of walking and steep climbs!

When the shed eventually lost its locomotives on 8 June 1929, engine driver Willy Wood remembered the last engine (Class 'J24' No 1893) leaving to be lowered down the incline for the last time. Willy remained at Rosedale upon retirement and was the last of the old NER Rosedale enginemen when he died here in 1963. A newly vacated NER cottage next to Willy's had been used by the YHA from 1933 until 1950 and is today one of those still occupied.

During rambles across these wild moors expertly assisted by Malcolm Dunnett, the Lion Inn, which so frequently in far off days provided a warm haven for snowbound Victorian railwaymen, again came to our assistance when the weather closed in unexpectedly and hail and sleet remarkably and suddenly obliterated autumn warmth and sunshine (as the photos testify!).

The Lion stands at an altitude of 1,293 feet and we recommend those interested to pause awhile here and view the old photos displayed commemorating the long-gone community, and a very civilised way it is to complete a long and enjoyable hike among Rosedale's railway 'ghosts'!

ROSEDALE ENGINE SHED: The shed, seen in 1932, three years after the lines were lifted and still awaiting demolition, had an allocation of five engines, which dropped in later years to three. Owing to the difficulties of lowering engines down the incline, repairs were carried out at the shed with, it seems, visiting fitters on occasions. When heavy overhauls became due, the engine was towed away to the incline top minus its middle pair of wheels to facilitate an easier get-away bearing in mind their weight. *JWA*

The present view, taken in November 1991, shows the general lie of the land with an indent remaining in the dale side where the shed out-buildings stood. *KG*

The shed was demolished in the mid-1930s and its stones can still be seen down in pretty Hutton-le-Hole as the basis for its village hall. However, the builders didn't require (or couldn't budge!) the great corner stones that once formed the shed door main stays. In the close-up shot (*left*) they are seen still bolted through with early iron bars, possibly originating from local ore, a poignant reminder of times past.

The other present-day view (*below left*) shows the loneliness of the vista as seen from above the old shed looking south. The form of the two filled-in inspection pits shows clearly and the remaining group of enginemen's cottages command fine views along the River Seven with the site of the Hollins Pit far below in the background. The course of the railway now forms a popular walkway. *Both KG*

BLAKEY JUNCTION (1): Our oldest view, taken *circa* 1890, is admittedly well known to avid Rosedale explorers, but had to be reproduced again as it so graphically portrays this strange gypsy-like railway community in almost frontier remoteness! Blakey is at a point where the Hutton-le-Hole to Castleton road once crossed the mineral lines via an overbridge (still extant today but filled in up to the remaining parapet and looking like a short wall). It was the remote setting for seven railway houses that also formed the 'block post' for the two routes here and we see a cheerful group of railwaymen with their wives and children enjoying a fine warm day; everyone, it seems, is engaged in a little 'front street' shunting! An NER 'birdcage' brake-van is seen at the rear of a train formed with traffic for Ingleby Incline (thence to Battersby). The Rosedale East Valley branch can be seen going off to the right, past the bogie-hut (and grounded coach) in the 'V' of the junction. The buffer-stop of one of the four sidings is being used to lean on, adding to the bizarre nature of this 'front street' highway! *KG Collection/courtesy of the National Railway Museum, York*

Today the light-coloured grasses form the tell-tale shape of the perimeter around what was the group of houses, whilst dark nettles and thistles cover the thinner soil of the contaminated house site. The light grass even extends around what was once the garden perimeter fence where, exactly 100 years ago, the smiling railwayman once stood proudly alongside his children. In the middle distance is the 'gap' where the line once passed beneath the road. The pathway extending around to the right leads towards a surviving one-wall relic, presumably a water-tank base. *KG*

BLAKEY JUNCTION (2): In 1950 John Armstrong recorded the situation at Blakey from the mound of earth that separated the two routes. The glimpsed group of houses look to be already in a sorry state, although the parked car may indicate that at least the farthest away (the one with the porch in the 1890 view) may still have been used. In the distance, at the point where the sidings merged with the running lines, a cairn of stones has been constructed - we were unable to find out why. *JWA*

In November 1991 even the pile of bricks that was once the bogie-shed for the linemen has been dispersed elsewhere. The site of the little group of houses where a few hardy generations of railwaymen were bred is now purged by the unceasing winds at 1,200 feet. All that remains is the post-railway cairn standing eerily alone in the gap that once carried the rails down towards Sheriffs Pit and the Rosedale engine shed. *KG*

Esk Valley

KILDALE is the first station east of Battersby and remains a popular stepping-off point for ramblers and cyclists alike. The circa 1950 view is of one of the inevitable Class 'A8' 4-6-2T locomotives as it awaits timetable time to depart towards Whitby. The rural charm of the station is quite clear; also noticeable is the original low platform recess immediately in front of the building. *JWA*

Regretfully this fine stone-built construction has been swept aside and the only remaining up-side platform accommodation is a bus-shelter-type waiting hut, appropriately greeting one of the troublesome 'Pacer' units in May 1989. Today the Whitby branch is served by a much reduced service of four trains each way, but the future of the line looks more positive in 1992, following proposals for a Middlesbrough-Grosmont summer shuttle service using minimal-cost Class '153' single-car units. *ART*

GLAISDALE: It is August 1953 and a late morning service from Whitby has pulled to a stand hauled by Class 'G5' No 67262. This lovely stretch through the Esk Valley was a favourite location for photographers when, in June 1975, BR allowed steam engines from the NYMR to run down to Whitby on a certain number of occasions per year. When maintenance parameters were dropped in line with lighter axleloads and cost economies, such engines became restricted, thus ending a happy time for NYMR business. *JWA*

Today's example of economy services and light axleloads is in the shape of a 'Pacer' set, a far better choice than no rail service at all. At the time of writing, the valley service is going over to single-car Class '153' units which can be coupled up for peak-summer strengthening. This November 1989 view is interesting because it shows that the recently closed traditional signal box has given way to driver 'DIY' methods, and this particular service is carrying three extra drivers who are learning to use the token exchange equipment housed in the cabinet. *KG*

STAITHES: We begin this section by returning to the Saltburn-Whitby line of the Whitby, Redcar & Middlesbrough Union Railway, opened to the public on 3 December 1883 and closed from 3 May 1958. Staithes is situated just outside the southern boundary of Cleveland and is undoubtedly the most unspoilt of the once numerous fishing villages that tucked themselves inside coves to get what little shelter they could from the elements, and possibly for other nefarious black market activities at one time! It can be seen that the ravine, worn away by the Roxby Beck, is deep and narrow and the tiered red-roofed cottages form a bizarre maze of twisting alleys leading down to the little harbour - it is a tourists' delight. It may be sheer nostalgia, but locals spoken to on our visit agreed that the presence of the 790-foot long and 152-foot high viaduct formed an integral part of Staithes. They feel its removal was perhaps a mite premature, although necessary from the cost and safety angle. Our past (1950) and present (1990) pictures do, perhaps, support their theory that a big something is missing, and we leave it to readers to decide upon the aesthetics - with or without? *JWA/KG*

Right The end of a grey, wet North Sea coastal day in the early '50s sees Class 'L1' No 67754 entering Staithes station off the single-track viaduct with a Middlesbrough-Scarborough stopping service. Staithes viaduct was the largest of the tubular viaducts on the route. Following diminished public confidence in viaducts after the Tay Bridge disaster, bracing was added between the piers and, because the wind could be as high here as on the Tay, a wind gauge (pictured) was fitted at the southern end of the viaduct, adjacent to the nearer signal-post in our view. Its working was simple. If the speed in knots reached a certain velocity, a bell rang in the nearby signal box and the 'job was stopped'! When the viaduct was demolished in 1960, the equipment was deposited in the NRM at York. *Both JWA*

KETTLENESS station attracted traffic and workers associated with the ore and alum mines in this area before the First World War. Afterwards there was very little to support station receipts and the migration to the towns/cities soon reduced the potential travelling public to 50! All hopes were pinned upon the tourist, and we all know what happened to travel habits after the mid-'50s. Our 1958 view is, in fact, the final day of passenger operations on this lonely, windswept plateau. Ironically called 'The Economist', a final Whitby-bound service awaits departure time whilst photographers swarm around to record the scene for the last time. The service was in the hands of the very capable Brighton-built 2-6-4 tank engines in its closing years, and No 80116 has the sombre job of writing the last page of the final chapter. *K. Linford*

The May 1990 view is remarkably unchanged, considering that 32 years intervene. *KG*

The view above, looking towards the crossing illustrated in the main pair of pictures on a dull, wet, blustery day in the early 1950s, serves to illustrate the 'garden shed' quality of the platform-based signal box, whilst Class 'L1' No 67764 wheezes to a halt, contributing to the low cloud base. Beyond the station lamp can be glimpsed the yard sidings, set at a relatively steep gradient to assist with gravity shunting in the absence of locomotion. Pictured right is the notice posted during the winter of 1957 announcing the line's demise. *Both JWA*

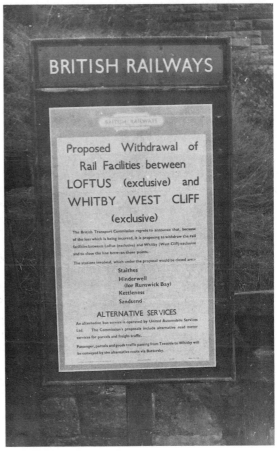

BRITISH RAILWAYS

Proposed Withdrawal of Rail Facilities between LOFTUS (exclusive) and WHITBY WEST CLIFF (exclusive)

The British Transport Commission regrets to announce that, because of the loss which is being incurred, it is proposing to withdraw the rail facilities between Loftus (exclusive) and Whitby (West Cliff) exclusive and to close the line between those points.

The stations involved, which under the proposal would be closed are:-

Staithes
Hinderwell
(for Runswick Bay)
Kettleness
Sandsend

ALTERNATIVE SERVICES

An alternative bus service is operated by United Automobile Services Ltd. The Commission's proposals include alternative road motor services for parcels and freight traffic.

Passenger, parcels and goods traffic passing from Teesside to Whitby will be conveyed by the alternative route via Battersby.

SANDSEND: In 1910 it is recorded that over 40,000 passengers booked journeys to/from this tiny station, but its heyday was fast approaching. From 1933 the northern limit of through running from here changed from Saltburn to Middlesbrough (via Nunthorpe), although in consequent summers some holiday trains reverted to using the Redcar route to Middlesbrough. This at least gave coastal travellers a direct service to the local capital. But from a service averaging six trains each way daily at the beginning of the century, it declined to three as the '50s progressed and the motor-car began to make its presence felt. The increasing cost of maintaining the five steel tubular viaducts and the bad weather exacerbated already plummeting receipts, and the service between Whitby and Loftus was withdrawn in 1958. The view opposite clearly illustrates the difficult and expensive engineering work (and its consequent high maintenance costs) as Class 'A8' No 69891 crosses the viaduct with a Middlesbrough-Whitby train in 1950. *JWA*

The lower view records the scene in May 1989; it can be seen that the station house is still prominent beside the viaduct abutment wall. The house in the foreground now has an attic extension and we thank the occupants for allowing us on to their property. *KG*

Above Sandsend Viaduct was the shortest of the five on the line at 268 feet, and its profile is well demonstrated in this 1959 view. *John Spencer Gilks/Ryedale AV*

Right These scenes of Sandsend will undoubtedly evoke happy memories for the many who were lucky enough to have had a holiday here, but special memories must belong to those privileged to have stayed in these perfectly situated camping coaches, glimpsed in the 1950 photograph and seen here in May 1957. *BR*

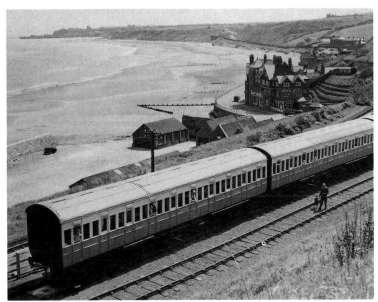

WHITBY, PROSPECT HILL JUNCTION: In such a photographer's favourite location as this, it was no surprise to find that John Armstrong had collected a large amount of material; we therefore hope that you agree with our selection. The oldest (upper) view is *circa* 1933 with Class 'A8' No 1529 (later 69876) hauling a Whitby-Scarborough service that would have had to reverse up from Whitby in the absence of an assisting engine being available. *JWA*

We next jump on 20 years to 16 August 1953, but find the scene little changed. The train is a Wakefield-Whitby-Scarborough Scenic Excursion and is longer than the previous train by two coaches. It has also reversed direction, having been manhandled up from Whitby by the pilot engine (still attached at the rear). Receiving help over these steep grades is the inevitable Class 'A8', this time No 69882 (ex-1503) accompanying more modern Class 'B1' No 61085. Facing the crews is the stiffest test of engine handling to be found almost anywhere - the climb up to Ravenscar. (We think we know which of the two engines would be the most sure-footed!) *JWA*

Wind the clock on a further 37 years (*above*) and both routes are gone. The Whitby-Scarborough section closed completely from 3 June 1965 and the through route beyond Prospect Hill, towards Whitby West Cliff station, four years earlier on 10 June 1961. The not inconsiderable engineering works hereabouts remain to amuse (and puzzle?) local people out walking their dogs. *ART*

The first railway to **Whitby** - horse-drawn - was the Whitby & Pickering Railway. Formed in 1832, the company was eventually up and running (or trotting) by 1836, but the technical and commercial pace was speeding up and by 1846 the redoubtable George Hudson had bought up the little company (for well in excess of the going rate) to ensure that his Y&NM-originating passengers did not have to endure horse-drawn speed on their last lap from York to Whitby Town. Hudson soon set about getting Whitby facilities shipshape and commissioned George Andrews, the York architect, to design an appropriate station, but this time more convenient for the townsfolk.

The first steam engine reached Whitby on 6 June 1847. The diversification of interest could not have come at a better time, for Whitby's main employment had long been associated with the maritime trade. Wooden ship construction - especially the wooden collier brigs - had nose-dived dramatically with the growth of the iron trade and ocean-going colliers of up to 20,000 tons, way beyond Whitby's depth.

A problem that was indirectly resolved by this maritime recession was the standage of empty railway stock. Up until 1900 train sets were towed out to places such as Ruswarp and Grosmont as the holding sidings opposite the MPD were limited. The problem was eased when the NER was quick to buy up the now quiet Bog Hall shipyard and began to construct not only sidings but also a new turntable.

The 1846-approved Esk Valley route was finally commissioned in 1865, and resulted in a new Whitby-Stockton service (via Battersby and Picton).

First to find a coastal road was the Whitby, Redcar & Middlesbrough Union Railway, when in 1883 operations began between Whitby and Loftus after some abortive construction work. Quickly following the WR&MUR came the Scarborough & Whitby Railway, which opened to business on 16 July 1885 and had itself encountered major engineering difficulties, being worked by courtesy of the NER from the outset. The Saltburn-Scarborough service experimented for many years with how best to include both Whitby stations, but never settled down to an ideal pattern. However, things changed dramatically when in the early 1930s the service was advertised as to and from Middlesbrough. From then on Whitby West Cliff was seen as the natural changing place for Town station, and no longer did through services attempt the much protracted business of including a call at Town. A regular shuttle up from Town to West Cliff was accommodated in additional bays outside the Town station train-shed and one at West Cliff, and became a very suitable shuttle service for the LNER's latest cost-shrinker - the steam railcar.

Apart from the First World War loss of the Whitby-Beck Hole shuttle service, the first major cut came in June 1954 when the Whitby-Stockton trains ceased with the abandonment of the Battersby-Picton section.

Next, on 5 June 1958, the WR&MUR route closed between West Cliff and Loftus, but the simultaneous introduction of DMUs (see Grosmont on page 112) meant that reversals on the line from Scarborough to Middlesbrough were immediately made easier, even though the trains were routed through circuitous Battersby.

Next to go, on 8 March 1965, was the pioneering section between Whitby and Pickering, with service curtailments to Malton and Scarborough. Broken now were Hudson's early plans, and after 118 years no longer could York travellers get to Whitby direct.

Enter the North Yorkshire Moors Historical Railway Trust - only time will tell if Malton will again be a junction. . .

WHITBY, BOG HALL JUNCTION: This was the point where trains from the two coastal routes joined the inland Esk Valley line (that is after successfully negotiating Prospect Hill's gradient!). Our first picture is thought to date from September 1958 and shows Class 'D49' No 62745 *The Hurworth* assisting an LM '4MT' train engine out of the stock sidings prior to propelling down into Whitby Town station to collect Midlanders going home on train M885. The 'D49' looks to be in poor condition and in fact lasted in traffic only a few months longer, being withdrawn in March 1959. *JWA*

Today's view shows the now simplified infrastructure adjacent to a public crossing that has seen many incidents over the years, but nevertheless still remains a right-of-way. When the Bog Hall slipways were acquired by the NER in 1901, the maritime fraternity feared that the still busy River Esk would be cut off by the railway, and insisted that pedestrian access be maintained. A Class '143' set makes for Middlesbrough with one of the four daily service trains in the autumn of 1990. *ART*

WHITBY TOWN (1): This view, commissioned by BR in March 1952, is a record of the 1847 structure, designed to George Andrews's orders, just nine months prior to the removal of the overall roof and cornice. The structure, which lasted 106 years, was built on a curve, it is apparently a typical Andrews design although in this case it had little to recommend - there were not only gauge problems because of the iron columns, but also the facilities annexed to the building were, from the onset, inadequate. From 1890 onwards, the clean external lines were ruined by the clutter of peripheral wooden buildings needed for the proper management of the station and for passenger comfort. The YNM had not even included a refreshment room in the plans, and yet the station was unusual in having the luxury of two portico entrances. Seen here is the support column that was subsequently altered due to gauge problems on the curve. Coach E87224 (labelled 'MALTON-WHITBY') stands in platform 2 below a loading gauge. In the bay adjacent is a teak-bodied vehicle. *BR*

Almost 40 years have rolled by in this October 1991 view of the same location. In 1953 this low cantilevered awning was erected, which meant the isolating of the upper part of the three large arched doorways that once led on to the platform. Today platform 2 is cut off from further train involvement, while platform 1 has a shortened face and is occupied by 'Pacer' set 143623 with a midday service for Middlesbrough. These days the townsfolk have a clearer view down into the station. *ART*

WHITBY TOWN (2): Seen from platform 2, a relatively new awning overlooks Class 'A8' 4-6-2T No 69852 of Middlesbrough depot. The driver awaits the 'nod' from the station staff with the West Cliff shuttle that acted as a feeder service to the coastal route (see page 98). *Ian Heyes Collection*

From today's surface of crushed limestone a single derelict stop-block with buffers acts as a leg-up to platform height. The 'Pacer' unit blends well into a Whitby Town station that was 'reopened' by the Town Mayor on 7 August 1991 after $3^{1}/_{2}$ million was spent on its modern multi-role adaptation to facilitate better community use with the addition of six shops into the former waiting room area. It is interesting to study the imposing town buildings from this viewpoint - note that the dominant central church has since lost its west-facing tower! *ART*

WHITBY TOWN (3): By the summer of 1959 DMUs had been travelling to Whitby for a year, but the coastal route to the north had gone and the unit seen here will reach Middlesbrough via Battersby (as will the 'Pacer' set in the present view). This picture portrays a nice assembly of the sort of power seen at Whitby as the '50s bowed out. The 'L1' tank No 67754 was a type from an earlier age and seems to be acting as the duty station pilot. The more recent 1954-built Standard 2-6-0 No 77012 stands at the head of a mixed van train, and semaphores seem to be everywhere. *Ian Heyes Collection*

In October 1991 we see the new, quieter face of Whitby Town. Railway property has been sold and replaced by this distinctive 'Lego' construction, whilst the wide platform retains the single concrete lamp post on the extreme left, alas with vandalised bulb cover! The midday service for Middlesbrough is just leaving. *ART*

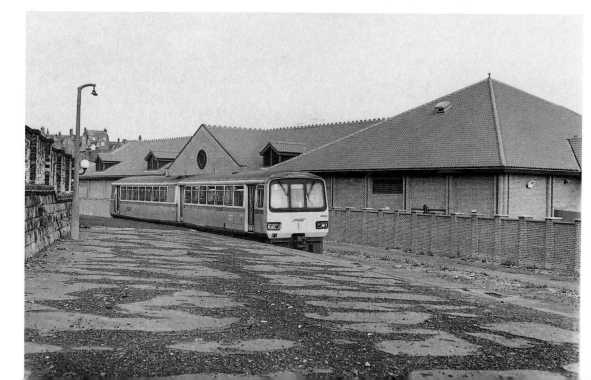

HAWSKER was the first station south of Whitby on the Scarborough & Whitby Railway and opened to the public on 16 July 1885. Together with Stainsacre it could only muster 400 potential travellers in 1911, but such were other methods of communication that almost a quarter of these people regularly used the station for one reason or another. Class 'A8' No 69879, then of Scarborough (50E) MPD, drifts downhill with a Scarborough-Whitby service into the station, to exchange single line tokens. *JWA*

Thirty-five years later, in March 1990, we were surprised to find the line is now sliced up into strips of back garden, and the station master's kitchen bay window has gone to make way for a radio receiving lean-to! The station closed (with the line) from 8 March 1965, and the only time the locals could remember the station being busy was when the Staintondale Hunt Point-to-Point Races were held here! *ART*

RAVENSCAR, WHITAKER'S BRICKWORKS: Looking from Crag Hall Lane bridge in the general direction of Fyling Hall Station, we see Scarborough Class 'A8' No 69867 shouting at the bleak coastal moors on its journey towards Ravenscar (and eventually Scarborough). The date is 16 August 1953. Of special interest at this point was the brickworks of Whitaker & Company with its kilns, chimneys and odd little ganister railway. The course of this narrow gauge railway can be seen going diagonally up the cliff towards the moors behind the tall chimney. Ganister (not used at the brickworks) was hauled by horse-drawn wooden wagons 1½ miles from Stony Marl Quarry and lowered to the Whitby line for transfer to NER wagons at Whitaker's Sidings. The story goes that on one occasion the cable snapped and the wagons hurtled across the lines and were lost at sea! This section of the S&WR knew many landslips; one incident in 1888 stopped the service for 12 days, and thereafter the NER began to pay particular attention to line-side drainage. *JWA*

The line closed from 8 March 1965 and today a tourist/ramblers' trail can be seen tamely passing the site of much past endeavour. *ART*

RAVENSCAR TUNNEL: The cause of so much trouble for locomen along this damp and (normally) windswept cliff-edge section of railway was Ravenscar (formerly Peak) tunnel, close to the summit of the Scarborough & Whitby Railway. Seen in the last few days of unrestricted photography - August 1939 - Class 'A8' No 1529 (later 69876) has no doubt earned the luxury of coasting through the 279-yard tunnel, with a further 3 miles down, all at 1 in 40, to Fyling Hall Station. To quote from Robin Lidster's book (see Bibliography): '. . . the railway was our lifeline . . . we often waited as the train came up from the bay after sticking in the tunnel after a sea-fret . . . once the loco crew were near suffocation after several failed attempts in the tunnel, and had to be revived with water upon reaching Ravenscar Station . . .' *JWA*

The tunnel today is just one of the interesting historical artefacts which make the Ravenscar-Robin Hood's Bay section one of the most delightful walks for either naturalists or local historians (but no excuse is needed!). *ART*

RAVENSCAR: Originally called Peak, the station was the summit of the line and the culmination of a 1 in 41 climb up from Ravenscar Tunnel. On 19 January 1959 this section caused the entire line to be closed due to a combination of mist, sea-fret and lack of use (the previous day being Sunday!). In July of the same year a Yorkshire 'Scenic' special on a round trip from the Leeds and Wakefield area approaches Ravenscar's level station area off the sharply contrasting rise from the tunnel. The leading engine is BR Standard Class '4' 2-6-4T No 80119, whilst the train engine is 'B1' 4-6-0 No 61069 of Neville Hill, Leeds. It is likely that the last vehicle is an observation coach. *JWA*

On 28 March 1990 one platform remains and the distant hotel on the horizon is a further reference point. There have been recent attempts to re-open a mile-long section of the line through Ravenscar in a scheme sponsored by a Wakefield coal company to the tune of £1 million for an engine shed (to house two locomotives), a new station, signal box, restaurant, car park facilities and the relaying of the line. The *Yorkshire Evening Post* of 9 May 1988 reported that the scheme had been vetoed by Councillors. The *Evening News* on the same date commented: '. . .wind causes too much disruption at Ravenscar', so the Scarborough Development Control sub-committee is recommending that the scheme 'be dropped'. *ART*

RUSWARP: For our final view in this section we return to the inland route up the Esk Valley towards Grosmont. Ruswarp and its associated villages of Sneaton and Stainsacre collectively produced a potential travelling public of almost 1,000 people in 1900. That the station was frequently used by a half of that number annually may have been in no small way due to its proximity to the River Esk and one of the few convenient crossing places. In our views of the bridge it appears to be supported by a collection of antiquated cast iron supports, but the truth is that the bridge is still adequate for the weight and low amount of traffic now passing. The August 1954 view shows, not surprisingly, an 'A8' No 69852. Originally a 4-4-4T Class 'H1' from Darlington Works in 1913, conversion to the 4-6-2T arrangement came in 1936 and with it a new lease of life. No 69852 was withdrawn in November 1959 and cut up at its birthplace shortly afterwards. *JWA*

The current view, taken on 30 March 1990, shows a Class '143' unit leaving for Middlesbrough. *ART*

North Yorkshire Moors Railway

Part of the Whitby & Pickering route of 1835-36, the Grosmont-Beck Hole section closed to passengers as early as September 1914, whilst the route known today as the preserved NYMR closed to all traffic from 6 March 1965. At a time when the aftertaste of Beeching was still fresh, re-opening closed railways was considered unfashionable, if not perhaps simply the ravings of idealists! Against all the odds, however, this railway did re-open - on 1 May 1973 - and was an example to many others showing what could be done by co-operation and determination.

The North Eastern Locomotive Preservation Group (NELPG) undertook to provide motive power to the North Yorkshire Moors Historical Railway Trust, and this arrangement, continuing right up to the present day, has gone from strength to strength, the line becoming a major attraction within an area of great beauty.

In the ensuing 25 years there have been some hair-raising financial moments when the founders sought backing and sponsorship during the early days of difficult negotiations. It is sad that some of the railway's entrepreneurs did not survive to see the 1992 Silver Jubilee.

An encouraging January 1992 press report stated that BR was looking at introducing a shuttle service dove-tailing into the NYMR timetable at Grosmont. Although BR will need Council funding to help support the costs, no one can deny that the NYMR is almost solely reliant upon the car to bring in passengers - and funds - and this joint venture can only be good news to those who put their money where their hearts are . . . in rail transport. It is to be hoped that a station-to-station shuttle bus link can be engineered at the Malton end, thus 'plugging in' the NYMR from both sides!

GROSMONT (BR): An early '50s view of the Whitby end of the station; the Malton pick-up (Class 'J25' 0-6-0 No 65663) is seen ambling along between vans on the goods road and highfits on the Battersby line. The station announces its platforms on the large orange NE area signboards. *JWA*

A little later, our second view shows the new down starting signal (replacing that on the bracket to the extreme left in the older view) awkwardly situated and almost in the middle of the platform. This was done possibly for improved sighting but was a considerable distraction to the unwary on a dark and foggy night! Some friendly rapport is exchanged between the porter and passengers, completing a delightful rural moment as the 'stopper' from Whitby arrives, the 'G5' Class No 67240 being dwarfed by its coaches! *JWA*

A fair-sized mound of stockpiled stones lies today on the signal box base, but the adjacent telegraph post has remained unmoved by all this activity. Beyond, the NYMR platform extension has crept towards the place where the brickworks once stood, while the sidings to the left into the gasworks have long since disappeared. 'WD' 2-10-0 No 3671 *Dame Vera Lynn* and the big 'T3' ('Q7') 0-6-0 No 901 (63460) are glimpsed on NYMR duty on 17 May 1991. *ART*

GROSMONT (NYMR) (1): On a summer evening in the 1950s Class 'A5' 4-6-2T No 69861 steams into the NYMR side of the station with a returning Whitby-Pickering train. *JWA*

A few years later, in 1957, this 'cats-whisker' Metro-Cammell DMU was still a novelty on the Whitby-Pickering route - but might this scene preempt eventual NYMR operations? *Ian Heyes Collection*

By May 1991 (*above*) the degree of change is not unnatural, but the discarded cable reel and timber oddments compare well with the early '50s pile-up of permanent way material stored on the up-side platform. The extended down-side platform is now the bi-directional platform for all services, and NYMR stock can now be seen stored along what was the Whitby branch proper. Where once No 69861 ambled through, today we see contemporary LNER Class 'T3' No 901 preparing for a run with John Dawson's rather fine clerestory saloon, a spectacular combination. Readers might be forgiven for confusing the past with the present! *ART*

GROSMONT (NYMR) (2): Grosmont Tunnel in 1956 gave John Armstrong a wide view over the station towards the junction. Arriving is a service from Malton in the charge of a BR Standard Class '4' tank, one of five received new from Brighton Works by Whitby shed during the previous year (and also destined to move on quickly). *JWA*

It makes a pleasant change to report on an altered situation showing even more steam activity, especially when it shows motive power more appropriate to a northern route; on 17 May 1991 the recently returned to service Class 'Q7' No 901 (better known to many as No 63460) is preparing to be on its best behaviour for a special invitation-only run hauling John Dawson's preserved North Eastern clerestory bogie coach. Itself possessing a history as complex as the powerful 0-8-0, it is affectionately remembered by everyone as the coach conveying the 'Old Gentleman' in the 1970 film of *The Railway Children*. The 'Q7' (LNER Class 'T3'), built during October 1919, was withdrawn on 3 December 1962 and put aside for preservation. On 12 August 1964 it went to Stratford for storage, eventually being hauled to the vacated Hellifield shed before returning south again to Brighton and finally, in 1978, back north into the NRM reserve collection at York. Its re-appearance in traffic marks ten years of restoration by NELPG and few will disagree that it has been well worth waiting for! *ART*

115

GOATHLAND SUMMIT (1): The 'past' picture of this pair smacks of a 'back to the future' twist considering that present NYMR/NELPG power includes apple green 'B1' No 1306! Sister engine No 61256, albeit in BR black lined livery, is shown passing the diminutive block post in 1955 whilst its custodian takes in the fragrance of the adjacent honeysuckle. *JWA*

Expected to be the most ambitious southern limit of the preserved line by the early NYMR members, the summit is passed today by trains *en route* to Pickering, the current southern terminus. Here in 1991 Class 'WD' No 3672 is close to the route of the popular Lyke Wake walk (Robin Hood's Bay-Osmotherley). The permanent way hut survives, although devoid of its creeping plant, and bears witness to a phoenix-like revival. *ART*

GOATHLAND SUMMIT (2): Slogging up to the summit in the opposite direction is another 'B1', this time No 61021 *Reitbok*. The 'B1' was making desperately slow progress but was obviously in the hands of a driver with the science and art of 'B1' manipulation finely tuned. It is probable that the many RCTS/SLS coach-bound observers still remember vividly the music from the engine as she constantly threatened to slip to a stand in appalling conditions. It can be seen that the steam sanders are hard at work on this 1 in 49 section.

Alan returned to find the same spot with no little difficulty. Due to permanent way work associated with the relayed section on view, it was a surprise to see *Dame Vera Lynn*, the big 2-10-0 engine, actually eased off over the gradient in marked contrast to the scene that had greeted him 28 years previously. Note that the mileposts remain behind the swathe of recently dug ditching in a happily unchanged view amid an attractive moorland setting. *Both ART*

Pickering from the Station.

PICKERING: A mid-1930s postcard shows the station under an impressive overall roof designed by Hudson's protégé George Andrews. *JWA Collection*

The station closed to passengers in March 1965, being subsequently re-opened by the North Yorkshire Moors Historical Railway Trust in May 1976. Today it seems a good example of 'modest' yet authentic preservation, when compared with the old postcard. The castellated tower in the background continues to look down upon developments here, as Brighton-built Standard Class '4' tank No 80135 enjoys an extended life on duties to which its sisters came new in the early 1950s. *ART*

PICKERING MPD began as a single-track shed to a design by George Andrews. Back in 1846 it measured 43 feet, in order to house one loco, that being the standard engine length of the day! By 1876 a length of 112 feet was the requirement; and the shed was extended. It went from housing bogie tank passenger 0-4-4Ts to 'G5s' (1923), 'N8s' (1934) and an 'N9' (1938), with the occasional 0-6-0 tender goods engine for limited country shunting activities. By the 1930s the depot also entertained one of the diminutive Class 'Y3' Sentinel locos, one remaining here until withdrawal in 1952. In more modern times a distinguished guest of three years was 'D49' No 62774 *The Staintondale*. It was eventually transferred away in 1951, the supply of spare parts having proved to be a problem. The last allocated loco, 'G5' No 67308 (see Malton MPD on page 131) was condemned and left the little shed in November 1955; thereafter engines were supplied from 'down the line' (Malton) until closures came in 1959. Here we see No 62774 on shed in 1950. *JWA*

The shed still stands today, and was photographed in the summer of 1991. But for anyone seeking to emulate our view, be warned - the shed is not easily found as it is cleverly integrated within a joinery firm, as seen here. Thanks to S. Taylor & Son for allowing access to their works. *ART*

Easingwold and Ryedale

Linking Easingwold to the ECML at Alne, 2¹/₂ miles distant, a short branch was launched in October 1887 and opened in July 1891, having enjoyed some lethargic management action!

To survive beyond nationalisation was a great feat for an 'independent', although it had become an official Light Railway as recently as 1928 further to reduce overhead costs. At that time staffing consisted of two drivers (who doubled as guards), one fireman, one station master, two clerks, four porters, two platelayers and the shed cat!

An uphill and extremely lucky struggle against the motor car menace went on from then until 1938 and, apart from a fictitious economic resurgence between 1940 and 1946, passenger receipts fell dramatically thereafter to reach a measly £18 total for the entire year of 1947. The hard decision was taken in 1948, and that became the last year of passenger traffic.

The company had its own engine, but the downturn of the late '40s also coincided with the loco's rapid deterioration. Thus by 1949, in order to maintain a goods service, the Easingwold Directors negotiated with BR for the loan of a small tank engine. This contract continued until complete closure in 1957, just long enough for the branch service to become a national oddity and the subject of much attention from the curious.

EASINGWOLD: Our 'past' view shows Class 'J71' No 8297, having recently arrived on hire from York shed and good value, even then, at £40 per week, seen outside her new temporary stable! *JWA*

In every book in this series there is at least one location that persistently defies capture. But Spennymoor old station site (see Past and Present No 4) was easy by comparison to this location! In spite of being well prepared with war-edition Ordnance Survey maps, AA guides and a compass, it still took much searching out during two weekend visits in August 1989. Altering the topography was the rapid growth of the large dominating tree completely mastering the old yew that is showing behind the shed in 1949. We hope readers agree it was worth the effort! *ART*

John Armstrong took the trouble to record the complete railway scene and pictured right we see the announcement telling the world that 'full truck loads' would no longer be made welcome at Easingwold from 28 December 1957. *JWA*

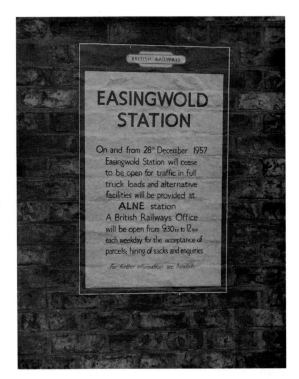

PILMOOR, SUNBECK JUNCTION: A little to the north of the Easingwold branch junction at Alne on the East Coast Main Line was the triangular junction at Pilmoor for the branch along Ryedale to Pickering. The southern junction on the ECML was controlled by Bishophouse Junction signal box, while the northern came under the aegis of Sessay Wood box. The junction of the two converging chords was here at Sunbeck, the place where you collected your token for the outward journey. In what is thought to be August 1949, Sunbeck's signalman, in shirtsleeves, meets 'Adex' (advertised excursion) No 265 off the north chord, and the fireman of Class 'V2' No 947 (soon to become 60945) leans down obligingly. The compulsory sleeper-built platelayers' hut is there, as is a small gas-lamp to illuminate the token-exchange platform. Formally opened on 9 October 1871 from Bishopthorpe Junction through to Gilling and Helmsley. Even when photographed, time was running out for shirt-sleeved days here, and the last train ran over the junction at Sunbeck on Saturday 31 January 1953. *JWA*

The footpaths still today mimic the north and south curves of the triangle, but of the signal box there is no trace. *ART*

SLINGSBY: At Gilling a branch ran off to Malton, a stretch of line whereon we found few train views perhaps due in no small way to the early (January 1931) withdrawal of the passenger service between Thirsk and Malton. Dating from 1853, Slingsby station was attracting 10 per cent of the potential travelling public in its catchment area by 1900; even though this was a good average figure, passenger potential was small and stretched to only five hamlets. The photo chosen from John's collection of prints is credited to a J. Hodgson of Cleckheaton, and we would wish to reimburse the present copyright holder - if known by any readers! The view is thought to be in about 1910 and shows NER Class 'A' 2-4-2T No 1598 with a train from Malton. *JWA Collection*

Because of trees, today's view bears little resemblance, but readers will notice that one distinctive gable end is featured, together with the castellated roofing plus chimney which have survived the ravages of time. The house is today a reception building for caravaners, and the large bay window facing the photographer is part of a cafe, a conversion from the single-storey building seen originally. Conifers hide other connections with the scene of almost 100 years before. *ART*

POCKLEY GATES CROSSING: Continuing along the line towards Helmsley, here is a frozen moment on an old world branch line where time had ceased to be the tyrant of enginemen, and the driver and guard often stopped to pass a few moments with a waysider, to share cakes (and ale?) and the latest rural news when perhaps running up to an hour before schedule! John Spencer Gilks provides proof that this way of life was not restricted to Irish byways by catching this charming moment in May 1960 as the driver of Class 'J39/2' 0-6-0 No 64928 (a long-serving member of Malton shed) opens the gates at Pockley Crossing to allow his lightweight Gilling to Kirbymoorside branch goods service to pass. The last regular passenger trains had been gone for more than seven years when this picture was taken. The line survived another four years until formal closure from 10 August 1964, the last goods pick-up service being on the Friday preceding, the 7th. *John Spencer Gilks/Ryedale AV*

Even though the concrete gate-posts survive and the spacious crossing-keeper's house is extended into a substantial property, the presence of electricity, vital though it is, has much changed the total scene, seen here on 28 March 1990. Trees have quickly plugged up the railway gap once seen in the distance, and old railway ballast comfortably forms a part of the farm trackbed. *ART*

SINNINGTON: Although this is one of John Armstrong's best-known photographs, we hope readers will excuse its inclusion in view of the many interesting details shown. Unfortunately Sinnington was in its death throes when he recorded the 10.23 York-Pickering service during the last day of passenger workings on the branch, 31 January 1953. It is appropriate for local Class 'D49' No 62730 *Berkshire* to perform the last duties. In his book on the railways of Ryedale, Patrick Howatt records the station as having 'one platform, signal box, cattle dock, horse dock, five-cell coal depot, weighbridge and weigh office . . .'. This leaves little doubt about the station's activities and it is no surprise that the chief goods business in 1924 was handling cotton cake, linseed cake and maize, all for the local mill belonging to the Turnbull family. *JWA*

The contemporary scene, in April 1990, shows a well-renovated station building, now an attractive holiday home. Thanks go to the proprietors, Mr & Mrs Allan, for allowing us on to their property. *ART*

PICKERING, MILL LANE JUNCTION: Part of the NYMR route of 1845, Mill lane Junction was 18 route miles from Gilling and was the diverging point for the lines to Scarborough and Gilling, east and west, from the Whitby-Malton main line. The route west was the last section opened from Gilling in 1875, the junction here formally clos-

ing on 2 February 1953. This delightful rural vignette of about 1950 shows Class 'G5' No 67273, with its new BR front numberplate, just after having slowed to collect the single-line token. The single coach looks particularly ancient. Of special note must be the arched chimney on the gate-keeper's cottage, supposedly a trademark of architect/designer G. T. Andrews who worked principally for companies controlled from York and has left his mark as recognisable features in the Yorkshire landscape. *JWA*

The Mill Lane of 4 April 1991 is unrestricted by crossing gates, and it can be seen that the crossing-keeper's cottage is now an integral part of orderly housing. It is almost obscured from view by a new dividing wall that has consequently separated the lineside bushes from the old cottage. We would like to acknowledge the help and assistance of Mr Jay, who allowed access to his property. *ART*

Malton area

MALTON STATION: Always the most important station between York & Scarborough, Malton served a population of over 10,000 people within a 7-mile catchment area. Opened with the line in 1845, the goods yard dealt in a good mixture of commodities (ale, flour and manure!) until quite recently, and in our circa 1952 photograph Class 'G5' No 67315 (at that time recently of Alston MPD) is shunting cask vans whilst Class 'B16' No 61414 of Neville Hill Depot (50B) passes with a Midlands holiday extra (No 324) bound for Scarborough. *JWA*

Today the platform is still in use but is the only one (now bi-directional) and it can be seen that the former island platform is now levelled ballast. The goods yard buildings are mainly still intact together with the water tank. The new face of Regional Railways is displayed by a 'Sprinter' unit on the Manchester-Scarborough run. *ART*

Above Not a practical repeat possibility, but nevertheless still a subject of special interest value - the moveable platform linking the down main platform with the up island structure. In Railway Stations of the North East (see Bibliography), Ken Hoole says that the '. . . station house and offices, all designed by Andrews, are accompanied by a train shed with an overall roof; originally it covered both up and down tracks and when the time came to widen them it was necessary to put the up platforms outside the south wall of the station, with passenger protection from the weather by an awning. This left a single track through the roofed section and this served the down platform; to reach the up platform a wheeled drawbridge (platform) was run across the down track, but this could only be done when no train was standing at the platform and when the [protecting] signals at the west end were at danger.' It was an unusual problem solved in an ingenious way and because, as Ken states, the moving platform was interlocked with the signalling the arrangement proved no threat to safe operations. *JWA*

MALTON EAST: The sinewy web of point rodding with its associated bell cranks and locking bars has now disappeared in the face of electrical relays and track circuitry of today's more recent signalling systems. Also gone are the heavy manual swing gates, so long a feature of this location and familiar to the many commuters who passed the spot daily. The signalman at least won't miss having to turn the gate wheel! Passing in good steam-tight condition in, it is believed, August 1953, is Class 'B1' No 61322, leading excursion No 58 with a very mixed scratch-set of excursion coaches. The train is bound for Scarborough and, hopefully, sunny beaches! *JWA*

Today's panorama, as seen on 3 June 1989, tells us that the up loop has gone amidst many detail alterations too numerous to mention. Industrially, the mill, once a source of much employment, has been transformed into small work units emphasising Malton's rural backdrop. Strange to relate, the signalman is also shown in the 'past' view at Rillington (page 134). Now approaching retirement, old photos caused his life to flash before him! *ART*

MALTON MPD: Across the running lines from the station and turntable was Malton locomotive depot. It had frequently been added to over the course of its early years, especially between 1865 and 1870; until that time 10 tank engines would, at a squeeze, get some cover! At its busiest, in the 1930s, 18 engines were allocated here, although it is known that Pickering and Whitby often acted as 'caretakers' for some of Malton's more complex cyclic diagrams (Pickering was a sub-shed up to Malton's closure in April 1963). In the older view, taken during the mid-'50s, the inevitable ex-NER Class 'G5' - this time No 67308 - is on show relaxing in the evening sun. *F. W. Hampson*

   Today's (April 1991) contrast is not what might be termed an aesthetic improvement, even though smokeless! *ART*

WHARRAM: On the Malton-Driffield branch dating back to 1853, Wharram surprisingly attracted as few as only 5 per cent of the travelling community at the turn of the century; this may, however, be explained by the rival station, Knapton, being on the more direct York-Scarborough route, and not too much further by pony and trap! Barley, wheat and oats kept little Wharram viable up until the Second World War, but with continuing poor passenger receipts, closure of the station was deferred only because of the war, and quickly followed in 1950. Goods and parcels traffic trickled on until complete closure in October 1958. Our 1949 picture of Wharram-le-Street shows the unusual house design. *JWA*

The 'past' picture proved of great fascination to the present-day inhabitants, who had found old views difficult to obtain. Wharram was visited in October 1991. *ART*

Above This early '50s view of the station exudes what was by then a 'freight only' atmosphere, with the station platform seating now removed and the distinctive shaped bush cut down and overtaken by weeds.

Below The location of this print from John Armstrong's collection had proved difficult to identify. A suggestion that it was Wharram was dismissed because the engine appeared to be about to pass John on a double-track station section. Further research, however, linked it with the view above, the limestone quarry buildings being just visible in both pictures. Thus we had discovered something so far elusive - a train at Wharram! The date is almost certainly 1951 or 1952, and we know that certain Filey Holiday Camp to Newcastle services were routed over this road to avoid Saturday bottlenecks.

One case in particular was the 08.55 from Filey calling at Bridlington at 09.25 then through to Newcastle, arriving at 13.12. Class 'B1' No 61068 would therefore avoid Malton station by taking the Driffield-Gilling route to slot eventually into the ECML via Sunbeck Junction (see page 122). How many Geordie holidaymakers today remember slipping past the abandoned halt whilst drinking their elevenses we wonder? Both these views were impossible to retake today because of trees and bushes. *Both JWA*

RILLINGTON: On the 1845 York-Scarborough line at a point just before the junction leading north-east from Malton to Pickering (and the NYMR) stands the country station of Rillington. Its most remarkable feature was the fine latticed iron train-shed roof, unglazed or untiled for many years, even when this mid-'50s photo was taken by John Armstrong. A relatively new build, and displaying the early 'lion and wheel' emblem, is Standard Class '4' 2-6-4T No 80118 leaving after a brief stop with a York-Whitby service. The signalman (also see Malton East, page 130) has just sent '2 bells' ('Train Entering Section') forward, and allows himself some moments to observe the train. *JWA*

In June 1989 the modern-day travellers on the Class '156' 'Sprinter' unit may briefly admire the well renovated station master's house before passing the rural station and its once thriving agricultural goods activity. The station back wall on the down side is the lone common reference point in this pair of photos. *ART*

Scarborough and Filey

NEAR SCARBOROUGH: The scene is about 1 mile out from Central station and 'B16' Class engines arriving up until mid-afternoon with early August Saturdays-only holiday trains passed by with almost boring regularity in 1959. This unidentified 'B16' coasts the last bit of the journey with its ten coaches from the Midlands.

By November 1990, a B&Q DIY store and indiscriminate bush growth are closing in upon the railway. The now empty salt bin on the left is almost lost opposite the surviving ³/₄ milepost at this point. *Both ART*

Scarborough, unlike Saltburn, was already an established resort before the coming of the railway, but its arrival spurred on much expansion. As elsewhere, railways caused considerable controversy at first and, reflects a Mr P. Dixon in his dissertation of 1965, 'Some even believed that in a few years the novelty of NOT having a railway would be one of the greatest recommendations of the town!' We suspect that there would be quite a fuss if BR attempted closure today.

In its excursion heyday, Scarborough had nine platforms and, from 1908, a tenth with the excursion platform at Londesborough Road. Trains arriving at the latter, after emptying, would draw forward through Falsgrave Tunnel along the Whitby branch to be accommodated out of the way beyond Belford Sidings at Gallows Close Yard (enlarged for this purpose in 1902) to be serviced, etc. All the track has gone from Gallows Close today, including the last stretch of the single-line Scarborough-Whitby railway; the last trader was a coal merchant. Falsgrave Tunnel was eventually filled to help adequately support the properties above who had endured many an earth tremor in steam days! Their lives are much quieter now.

As a footnote, let us place on record the thanks of all steam enthusiasts to Scarborough Borough Council for their financial assistance in getting world-beater No 4468 *Mallard* up and running for those magnificent World Record 50th Anniversary runs in 1988.

SCARBOROUGH (1): We are still 200 yards from the station, yet a platform end is already in view! This was the Whitby line platform and its history is interesting. Whitby trains originally used the set-back station facilities, arriving by the track approaching the camera on the left. These services then had to stand whilst their engines ran round to pull the stock into the station, and naturally this operation was fouling other movements. The authorities therefore extended platform 1 in 1934 to make 1A (the buffer-stop position of which is seen in the 'present' view overleaf). This gave Whitby services a less calamitous presence - they simply slipped down from the tunnel, stood for a short moment, then were signalled back into 1A via an especially authorised propelling movement. This 1950 view from adjacent to the tablet-catching platform exudes that definitive holiday casualness found in these places. Class 'A8' No 69867 has recently propelled back into 1A and those who have detrained mingle with local 'spotters' whilst the guard chats to the footplate crew. *JWA Collection*

Falsgrave signal box (also the name of the tunnel on the Whitby line) is still there today and, together with the overall gantry, adds distinction to a truly Victorian view not diminished at all by the presence of what is almost 21st-century technology in the form of a Class '158' from Manchester. *ART*

SCARBOROUGH (2): In 1959 Alan Thompson managed to 'snap' 'D49' No 62739 *The Badsworth* from the last coach of his York-bound train during what can be seen to be a delightful summer evening at Scarborough. Over to the right is a large sign to warn passengers that they had almost arrived, and the station is glimpsed alongside the signal box beyond the overbridge.

Today's view, taken from the still extant, but rail-less, Whitby platform (hidden from view in the past picture) is unmistakably the same place, although it may be that less of the grand Victorian housing is used as family accommodation these days! It is October 1991 and it is 31 years since *The Badsworth* was able to pollute the air (she was withdrawn in October 1960). It can be seen that the station signal box has gone and the station operates on a reduced format now that platforms 6 to 9 have been cleared and the track removed. The train shed here now protects cars, not passengers. Our picture shows a 'Pacer' Class '144' unit leaving for Hull. *Both ART*

SCARBOROUGH CARRIAGE SIDINGS: South of the station and shed area lay the main carriage sidings for, in particular, the summertime excursion stock, lying on the green-belt fringe of the town. It is 1959 and a Class 'K3' is gainfully employed on something other than freight haulage with excursion stock from the East Midlands. It is Doncaster's (at this time) No 61961 and some 'wag' has added the legend 'TOWING' to the smokebox door! At the extreme left, working that day as pilot engine in the carriage sidings, *The Badsworth* is seen again.

Thirty years later, in July 1989, Alan returned to the same spot, a little older and much wiser! The old gatekeeper's cottage can be seen incorporated within a market-gardening centre, while the carriage sidings are now the home of Payless DIY. It must be quite surprising to readers to that the NER trespass sign survives as a time-link. *Both ART*

SCARBOROUGH MPD: On 25 May 1952 No 45705 *Seahorse*, then of Farnley Junction, is seen on Scarborough shed having very likely brought in one of the frequent Manchester excursions. This particular view belies the spread of the shed area which, because of its situation constrained between the main running lines and Seamer Road, made up in length what it lost in width. The roundhouse shed that was completed in 1882 lay further to the north and much closer to the excursion platforms at Londesborough Road, which were built on the site of the very first Scarborough shed of 1845 (demolished about 1906) which by 1890 had been eclipsed by two other sheds, the roundhouse already mentioned, and an eight-road dead-ended shed, shown here. The roundhouse gradually fell into disuse and until closure in 1963 latterly became a dead engine store. This left the illustrated eight-road straight shed as the principal player. Subsidence in 1959, however, blighted its future prospects and large timber baulks shored up the end walls to give the operations department time to plan alternatives. The shed was demolished soon afterwards. *JWA*

The view from Seamer Road in October 1991. A 'Pacer' set skitters past the site of thousands of spotting hours with a Scarborough-Hull service. *ART*

Right Midway between the two main shed complexes in the late 1950s is Class 'D49' No 62717 *Banffshire*. No 62717 went to Gateshead shed in January 1951 to liberate sister No 62743 to Haymarket (the first 'D49' 'Hunt' engine to have a permanent allocation in Scotland). No 62717 thereafter never strayed from the NE area until withdrawal in January 1961. Her life mileage was 972,064. *ART*

Right A reminder of happier times at Scarborough in the summer of 1952. The driver of York-based modified Class 'B16' No 61472 cautiously observes the point blades as he leaves the area 'twixt sheds (the roundhouse shed behind) to back on to his train. The 'Flyer' was the prestigious Restaurant Car Express with through carriages to and from Whitby; the up and down trains passed in the vicinity of Hadley Wood each Saturday of the summer season. It traditionally left Scarborough Central shortly after 10.00, arriving at King's Cross at about 15.00. *JWA*

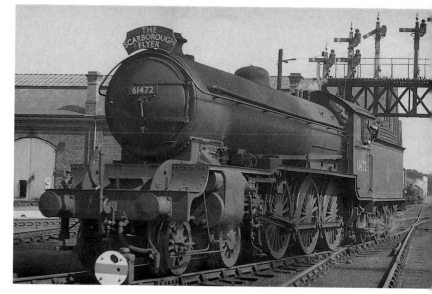

Filey station roof has been the subject of a long-running saga between BR and Scarborough Council, which began in 1988 when BR sought consent to demolish the Grade 2 listed roof. Scarborough naturally refused point blank and thus began a classic 'Catch 22' situation that BR finds increasingly frustrating whilst also trying to run a railway!

The problem was that the old roof was becoming increasingly dangerous with repairs urgently needed, whilst the protocol for each tiny repair job was to seek out planning approval *before* action. Delays in getting approvals meant increases in costs, with such expenditure unjustified if based upon the receipts of the halt. BR thus went cap in hand to several societies for financial help, but cash was dependent on BR also making good entire roof sections that had been removed - for safety reasons - 20 years before. BR was thus in an invidious position, and had to find a crock of gold before even small contributions became available. The most financially sensible option of complete removal having been refused, BR had to repair the structure - piece by piece - under the critical eye of English Heritage personnel.

Given the present condition of the roof, the repair work would cost £1/4 million, but to qualify for any money BR must also replace the hip ends as seen in our 'past' view, together with the lantern apex, thus bringing the cost to half a million. By the time

this book appears all the essential repairs will have been undertaken and possibly the hip replacement work begun. The completed work will then be enjoyed by the community in the same way as Redcar, as the finished structure will encompass a development of shops, offices and craft centres, and a joint partnership scheme is also under consideration with the Local Authority.

Filey is one of the few remaining two-track through stations with a single-span wrought iron roof, and designer and engineer George Andrews would no doubt be surprised at the consternation his work has caused to so many people!

FILEY: The summer of 1955 sees holidaymakers, national servicemen and a few curious children observing the arrival of a midday additional at a time when Filey would see 350 trains a week and an average of 8,000 passengers daily! Constructed by the Hull & Scarborough Railway and opened for traffic by 1846, our earlier view gives a glimpse of characteristic architecture in the Andrews mould. Note that the footbridge (added later) was designed to fit snugly within the side wall parameters but, because of its standard design it had to poke through the wall and turn back inwards to reach the platform (on the left). *JWA*

Doncaster-based Class 'B1' No 61145 has by 3 June 1989 metamorphosed into an ageing 'Heritage' Class 108 DMU on a Scarborough-Hull train; it is sobering to think that these two types will have rubbed shoulders on active service at another place prior to 1966! The water-tank base remains, as do the concrete station name-board supports over on the down-side platform. The Scammell tractor and the Norton motorbike very definitely belong to another day. . . *ART*

INDEX OF LOCATIONS